5 HABITS
OF THE TECH-READY
FAMILY

CHRIS MCKENNA

Founder and CEO of Protect Young Eyes

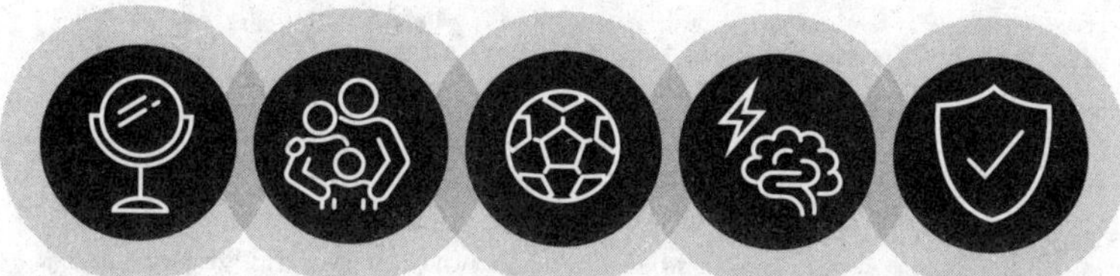

5 HABITS
OF THE TECH-READY
FAMILY

RAISING WISE KIDS IN A
WILD DIGITAL WORLD

ZONDERVAN BOOKS

ZONDERVAN BOOKS

5 Habits of the Tech-Ready Family
Copyright © 2026 by Chris McKenna

Published by Zondervan, 3950 Sparks Drive SE, Suite 101, Grand Rapids, MI 49546, USA. Zondervan is a registered trademark of The Zondervan Corporation, L.L.C., a wholly owned subsidiary of HarperCollins Christian Publishing, Inc.

Requests for information should be addressed to customercare@harpercollins.com.

Zondervan titles may be purchased in bulk for educational, business, fundraising, or sales promotional use. For information, please email SpecialMarkets@Zondervan.com.

ISBN 978-0-310-37128-1 (audio)

Library of Congress Cataloging-in-Publication Data

Names: McKenna, Chris, 1974- author
Title: 5 habits of the tech-ready family: raising wise kids in a wild digital world / Chris McKenna.
Other titles: Five habits of the tech-ready family
Description: Grand Rapids, MI, USA: Zondervan Books, [2026]
Identifiers: LCCN 2026004158 (print) | LCCN 2026004159 (ebook) | ISBN 9780310371250 trade paperback | ISBN 9780310371274 ebook
Subjects: LCSH: Internet and children—Safety measures | Internet and teenagers—Safety measures | Internet and youth | Parenting
Classification: LCC HQ784.I58 M397 2026 (print) | LCC HQ784.I58 (ebook)
LC record available at https://lccn.loc.gov/2026004158
LC ebook record available at https://lccn.loc.gov/2026004159

Cover design: Micah Kandros
Cover illustrations: Shutterstock
Interior design: Denise Froehlich

Printed in the United States of America

26 27 28 29 30 LBC 5 4 3 2 1

To my family. Andrea, Lauren, Cole, Grant, and
Blake, you are more than I deserve.
Thank you for allowing me to practice much of this "on you."

Contents

Introduction

Nothing vast enters the realm of mortals without a curse.

—Sophocles

I must post something.

I had that thought—a pressing, anxious thought—*while* writing this introduction. And I'm ashamed to admit that it required willpower to stay the course and keep writing. Like "the one ring to rule them all," my phone exerted a tractor-beam tug on my attention, making it difficult to focus.

Wait. I'm an adult! I'm *supposed* to have a brain that allows me to stay on task and write.

Aren't I?

Sir Tim Berners-Lee, the humble software engineer who invented the World Wide Web, envisioned something radically different: an open, free, and empowering "canvas for humanity."[1] When I met Sir Tim at the World Economic Forum, his hopes remained the same: The internet *should* serve as a tool of collaboration, not exploitation, and a space of trust, not manipulation.

But here's the question: When you open your phone in the morning, do you feel like you're stepping into a gift . . . or a curse? Do you feel more connected, more informed, and more free? Or do you feel overwhelmed, manipulated, and even diminished?

If you're a parent, you feel the fragility of this "gift." And our children do too.

Jordan DeMay was a high school senior in Marquette, Michigan, looking forward to graduation and a future in college. He was a popular student and homecoming king who enjoyed football and basketball and had a loving, attentive family. His parents, John and Jennifer, did everything they knew to protect him regarding technology. They monitored his accounts and spoke openly to him about dangers.

On March 24, 2022, Jordan received an Instagram direct message (DM) from a girl named Dani who wanted to be friends. She seemed nice, was pretty, and had mutual friends with him. After earning Jordan's trust, she requested nude photos, and he complied. The combination of arousal, pressure, ease, and a brain driven by feelings (like all teen brains) created an overwhelming, toxic force—even for a "good" boy such as Jordan.

But this was no teen girl. Brothers Samuel and Samson Ogoshi, part of a Nigerian-based criminal network called The Yahoo Boys, were operating a hacked Instagram account and demanded $1,000 from Jordan. They threatened to send the explicit images of Jordan to his friends and family if he did not pay—a devastating thought to Jordan since he lived in a small town. The Ogoshi brothers leveraged Jordan's distress with evil taunts and pressured countdowns such as, "I'll send it in ten, nine, eight . . ."

After Jordan paid $300, he threatened to kill himself. The brothers responded: "Do that fast . . . or I'll make you do it . . . I swear to God." Jordan died by a self-inflicted gunshot wound a mere six hours after the Ogoshi brothers had begun talking to him—a beautiful future wiped away by financial sextortion.[2]

It's hard to start off with Jordan's tragic story. It's our worst fear, illustrating what we're striving to protect against. Admittedly, no amount of conversation, software, or monitoring can guarantee zero digital problems in an era of vast technology. But I firmly believe that parents who have the right mix of being observant, engaged, and informed are often successful in favorably tipping the odds to their side. And thousands of families have testified to this (you'll read their stories throughout this book). Our job here is to decrease the probability of "the curse" so that your home and family are ready for the boundless technology being used. You will then be able to protect without panic and train without fear, donning your cape of newly discovered digital superpowers.

You might be thinking, *Chris, I don't know what to say! I don't know how to talk about sextortion, porn, or predators. When my kids want to play at their friends' houses, I'm afraid to talk to their parents about it. And I don't even know where our router is, let alone how to filter the dumb thing.*

Keep going! These chapters are your guide. Digital confidence is within your reach.

———————

Ironically, technology almost ruined me and destroyed my marriage. But in the words of Pastor Jacob Aranza, "Sometimes God turns our misery into powerful ministry."[3]

Have you ever been burdened by something you just couldn't shake?

I was on a typical evening run near my home about eighteen years ago, heading down a street I had covered hundreds of times over the past year. But on that specific block of sidewalk on that specific night, while listening to a sermon by Matt Chandler, a holy conviction struck me: It was time to tell my wife my secret.

I was looking at porn.

I had found a stack of magazines when I was around eight years old. Where and how isn't important, but I know what I saw, and it stirred an unhealthy curiosity that I didn't understand. So, as a child, I buried it like a landmine, waiting for a trigger. For me, that trigger was the 1990s internet when online porn arrived with Netscape like an uninvited plus-one. It's often said that as soon as we make an advance with media, we pornify it. And I struggled to handle the unfettered access that this new internet afforded me.

Dr. Alvin Cooper was a clinical psychologist who authored the groundbreaking work *Sex and the Internet: A Guidebook for Clinicians*. He described three forces unique to the internet that combined to create "a powerful attraction for individuals" known as the *Triple A Engine*.[4] The three A's in the Triple A are a combination of Accessibility (constantly available), Anonymity (a toxic secret), and Affordability (free), which accelerated compulsive online sexual behaviors. This became a problem for my brain. While watching porn, I was a distracted, less committed, unfaithful version of a father and husband. But I couldn't see it because we almost never see our own issues objectively.

I pride myself on having a strong work ethic and for being a self-starter:

- valedictorian of my high school class
- varsity athlete
- *summa cum laude* and Presidential Scholar in college
- fluent in a foreign language
- accomplished CPA and business adviser for Fortune 500 companies
- father and loving husband

But I was powerless against porn. It ruled me. I tried to stop so many times. But although I experienced temporary victories, porn always came back—*WHAM!* Like a bloodthirsty lion, the urge to click through endless online images and videos devoured my will and I was powerless. It controlled me. Trust me—I desperately wanted to stop, but I couldn't. Unlike just about everything else I had set out to do in life, I discovered that *my* strength was just not enough to overcome porn.

I did not find freedom until encountering the Holy Spirit on that evening run, coming clean to my wife and a couple of close friends, and using accountability software (thank you, Covenant Eyes).

But about five years after my battle, I watched us put that same monster—the internet—in our children's pockets. I watched kids start to *carry* the exact snake that bit me, and almost no one at our church seemed nervous about this. I wasn't just concerned about kids having access to porn. There was just no freaking way the thirteen-year-old version of me could have handled a hundred million choices to *anything* in my pocket. Could you have handled this?

At that time, I didn't have the studies to back up this uneasiness. Vindicating research and books on the topic, like *iGen* (Dr. Jean Twenge, 2017) and *The Anxious Generation* (Dr. Jonathan Haidt, 2024), were still years away. But something terrified me about what we were doing, especially when I considered what I had experienced *as an adult*.

I had to do something.

Enter youth ministry—the last place anyone expected to find me at that point in my professional journey. In 2009, I traded my twelve-year consulting career and a senior management title at EY for a role leading junior high students at our church. On paper, this made no sense. But the pull was unmistakable, and every sign pointed in the same direction. So I went that way, even without health insurance.

For the next seven years, I poured my heart into a large middle school ministry. I adored this age group in all its messy, loud, and audacious glory. But around 2014, something began to shift. At that time my lost-and-found box overflowed with Bibles, coats, and hoodies from youth group. No one ever left behind their new prized possession: the hand-me-down iPhone from their parents, who were unknowingly navigating a massive education gap. I had fought my own battles with temptation, but parents had zero idea that porn was three taps away on the iPhone 5 that they had just handed their child (parental controls barely existed back then). It was becoming clear that *few to none* of the parents in our church were using Instagram themselves. If they had done so, they would have seen what I did: easily discoverable pornographic images and videos as well as men actively soliciting young girls and selling explicit images of children. An informal poll of two thousand teens conducted by my friend found that 75 percent were receiving unsolicited DMs from strangers.[5] After setting up some test accounts pretending to be twelve-year-olds on Instagram, I received explicit images such as men masturbating and links to porn. The money scams were endless. These were the early, completely unfiltered wild days of social media, and they were *horrifying*.

With this backdrop, our head of adult discipleship mentioned in passing during one staff meeting that there was an open week in the teaching calendar, and she didn't have anything for the adults.

I had an idea. I raised my hand.

"Can I talk to parents about online porn?" I asked. This was 2014—a time when few churches spoke openly about porn.

Amazingly, I was given the green light to present my talk, "Digital Kids and Online Porn," to about seventy-five parents. Honestly, I half expected them to bolt for the exits. But something amazing happened instead—nobody left. In fact, they leaned in, hungry for more.

Sensing their eagerness, I invited them into a private Facebook group that I called Digital Kids. There, I began posting PDFs packed with the latest apps and online dangers that kids were facing. The parents devoured every word like it was a survival guide. They had not previously known that any of these "fun apps" could exploit their kids.

Just four months later, tragedy nearly struck. A local teenage girl was almost abducted through the Kik app, which is widely known as a platform for predatory activity. Suddenly, this wasn't theoretical anymore. Our local FBI office urgently needed someone to help warn parents across West Michigan, and the lead agent was coincidentally a friend from church. A whirlwind followed. Right after the 2015 Super Bowl, the local news ran a five-day series with me about digital risks, catapulting the issue into the spotlight.[6] Local parents started clamoring for more information. In that moment, my mission became crystal clear: to arm as many parents as possible with the truth about this new digital minefield. A few months later, I launched a website—Protect Young Eyes—and the journey truly began.

I started saying *crazy* things to parents, such as "Don't give kids smartphones or social media until at least age fifteen." Some parents didn't understand what the fuss was about. Snapchat and Instagram are just pictures, right? Musical.ly (TikTok's predecessor) is just fun videos, right?

But others started flooding me with their stories. During one talk at a medium-sized church, I shared very openly about my personal struggles with pornography in a room with a hundred parents. When I finished, they rushed to the stage to share their own anecdotes, expressing a liberating feeling that someone was talking about this, something they hadn't experienced before.

I knew we were onto something.

I want to share a favorite example from our parent presentations. I call it the "Did your mom ever put porn in your backpack?" illustration, and it's a powerful empathy builder.

Imagine it's a typical morning of your seventh-grade year. (Some of you just shuddered, recalling one of the most awkward, confusing, dramatic, depressing, exciting, and *weird* years of your life.) It's morning, and you just finished two perfectly toasted Eggo waffles and juice.

You grab your backpack—but before you leave, your mom says she has a few things to give you for the day.

You have an amazing mom—she's loving, but strict. So, here's what she does. She takes that backpack and puts in:

- a notebook, your pencils, your history book;

and

- a DVD player, plus movies—tons of them;
- a small television—the one with the DVD player in the front;
- a Walkman, plus your CDs—like, all of them;
- a radio;
- the Nintendo and your favorite games;
- a digital camera;
- pictures of all your friends;
- *MAD* magazine;
- Pokémon cards;
- your Ken Griffey Jr. rookie card;
- a basketball; and . . .
- five porn magazines.

She zips everything up and says, "Don't touch anything other than the notebook, pencils, and history book—all day. And I know most of your friends also have all these entertaining things in their backpack. But even though their parents don't care if they play the Nintendo, operate the camera, or even look at porn, you're not allowed to use any of their things either. Not during the day, nor on the bus. Oh, one more thing: If you *do* touch any of those things that are so fun, engaging, and intriguing in your backpack, you're grounded for a month. Got it? I hope you have an amazing day at school!"

This seems like nonsense! But is it? Because that's the analog equivalent of handing your child a smartphone today. *We ask our children to exert a level of self-control we simply never had as children.* This is why I often say, "It's not their fault" throughout this book. It's not because I'm relaxed about consequences—it's to remind ourselves of how it feels to walk around as a kid today with godlike technology in their pocket.

So, how do we handle this? How do we even begin to think about it?

Let's take a cue from the Bible.

In the opening lines of his Gospel, John gave us a picture of Jesus that is as revolutionary as it is practical: *"full of grace and truth"* (John 1:14). And notice the order: grace first, then truth. This is no accident—John wanted us to see that Jesus leads with compassion, then follows with conviction.

Now fast-forward to your living room today. If there's a device in your home connected to the internet, including that smart TV glowing in the corner, your amazing child is walking through a minefield. Unlike the childhood many of you experienced, where seeing something explicit required extensive planning and sneakiness, the odds of your child stumbling into something destructive aren't just possible; they're almost inevitable.

But here's the thing: It's not their fault. Kids are wired for curiosity, for risk, and for dopamine-fueled thrills. And digital platforms built by some of the sharpest minds on the planet are designed to exploit exactly those instincts.

So, what's a parent to do? *Grace first.* Meet them the way you long for Jesus to meet you in your mess—steady, patient, forgiving. *Truth second.* Spell out the boundaries, name the consequences, and, yes, take the phone when you need to. But never flip the order.

Don't ever take for granted what we're up against: Your child is battling MIT-trained software engineers who spend their careers figuring out how to capture attention *and* affection. Our kids don't stand a chance alone. And their hearts are no match for a parent who responds with nothing but frustration. *Grace first*—because when empathy runs high and anger stays low, something beautiful happens.

Your kids will stay close. They'll stay connected. Even when the pull of technology is strong, the stronger pull will be toward *you*.

Let's Give Our Kids Superpowers, Instead!

I always thought I'd be a partner or CFO in a financial firm by now. But in 2015 a website intended to help a few parents at my church became a call to help millions of parents around the world. Protect Young Eyes (PYE) is now a full-time calling—a small team intent on showing families step by step how to raise tech-wise, morally grounded, and resilient kids with grace and grit. The drive behind PYE is my relentless desire to give *you* tools that will:

- prevent tech from disrupting and ruining childhood innocence
- encourage your children to gaze up, reach out, and experience the heck out of this world
- stop your son or daughter from becoming a twelve-year-old version of *me*: powerless against digital addiction that's coming for them

I've mentioned that I'm a former youth pastor, so I come at this from a biblical worldview that deeply desires human flourishing. Even if that's not your worldview, we all want our kids to flourish. Don't we?

We can't wait for institutions to help. Companies, Congress, classrooms, and places of worship continue to fail our children in digital spaces. This means it's up to *us*—parents, caregivers, and grandparents! It's up to *us* to protect this #onepreciouschildhood and prepare our kids to encounter a digital world that's hungry for their hearts and minds.

Together, we can do this. Those who have persevered through the pressures and persistent kid requests have seen the benefits firsthand.

I shared this testimony on Instagram:

Every day we hear stories from parents whose children have started secondary (school) without a smartphone this year and are thriving. As one teacher told us last week, "You can tell instantly which kids don't have one, because it's like they've got a secret superpower compared to their peers. They can concentrate, they can hold a conversation.[7]

A teacher from Australia commented:

As a middle school teacher, you can 100 percent tell, and the guts to say no is such a phenomenal gift to give your child![8]

Another left this comment:

I work in early childhood education (infant–5yrs) and it's very easy to tell how much screen time kids get at home and what kind of shows they watch just by observing how they interact with their environments.[9]

I once received an email from a college freshman whose parents didn't give her social media until well into high school. This decision had a profound impact on her life:

My parents used your PYE tools and advice to raise me into someone who, in return, is advocating for more transparency on the issue of child sexual abuse material throughout the world.

She's now graduating from college and is on my board of directors! The digital risks that come with "yes" far outweigh the risks that come with "no" and "slow." If you've already given away too much access, don't despair. It's not too late to lead with relationship, talk about changes you want to make, and reestablish boundaries (I'll explain how to do this). If your kids are still little, I'll show you how to start strong, stay strong, and think long-term. I want you to experience the confidence of being a *steady* digital parent *ready* to prevent and identify problems, say the right things at the right time, and be able to respond with grace and calm when something slips through.

———

It is unreasonable to pit our children against the world's most sophisticated technologists. It is equally insane to expect us parents to simply "figure it out" while facing technology that permeates friendships, sleepovers, classrooms, homework, sports teams, youth groups, and even the bus ride home. This book exists to correct that imbalance, equipping you with the clarity and tools needed to prepare and protect your family online.

If the rapid pace of technology has left you uncertain about how to think—much less how to act—this book offers a path forward. It will help you develop an informed *way to think* and cultivate new habits for *what to do*. Both matter, because behavior follows belief.

We'll start by diagnosing our current parenting condition. What in the world is going on, and how did we get here? Then we'll dive straight into the Five Habits of a Tech-Ready Family—one chapter for each Habit—where you'll read stories from the trenches (real conversations with parents), learn our best tips honed from thousands of conversations, and see the Habits in action.

Five Habits of the Tech-Ready Family

- Habit 1: Model the right behaviors.
- Habit 2: Pursue authentic connection.
- Habit 3: Encourage work and play.
- Habit 4: Delay addictive technologies.
- Habit 5: Diligently prevent harm.

Habits 1 and 2 are built on strengthening the *relationship* between you and your child. We'll talk about how those Habits are the foundation for everything going forward. Habits 3 and 4 are built on *mindsets* and *knowledge* that empower us to push back on culture. These Habits give us the empathy and understanding necessary to courageously confront the narrative that technology is inevitable. And Habit 5 is the nitty-gritty. We'll get specific and stepwise about modems, routers, filters, apps, and tools that you may not have known about, all designed to protect your kids. You'll leave with names, details, and an action plan for harm prevention.

Since you're a busy parent, at the end of each Habit chapter I'll give you the five most important things to remember and revisit, as well as two simple steps you can take *this week* to see real progress in building a tech-ready family. And if you'd like to go on this journey with others, I invite you to join us at the Tech-Ready Family website, where you can download small group dis-  cussion questions (the chapters divide up nicely into weekly sessions) and prayers to keep you going. A lot is riding on you, and you need support.

Maybe you're a "Chief Technology Officer" mom, in charge of keeping your kids safe on the daily. Maybe your kids are still little and you're "getting ready." Maybe you're a grandparent feeling clueless while raising digital-native grandchildren, which is increasingly common. Maybe you're a new foster parent feeling completely run-down and overwhelmed by the task of raising your new daughter and her tech.

Perhaps you're even struggling to get a handle on your own digital life.

In the chaos of AI, YouTube, Instagram, fake news, brain rot,[10] Roblox, and TikTok challenges, let this book be your anchor.

While the internet has some positive aspects, quite a bit of it *isn't* better for us or our kids. We probably don't distrust social media enough. Young humans demand visceral experiences to develop properly, just like Grandma would have said. Childhood is for wiring the brain with tons of movement because brains are *built*, not *born*.[11] These experiences include skinned knees, paper books, eye and skin contact, and holding pencils and crayons. Yes, *some* tech is part of childhood. But something to feel, something to touch, and someone to hold is more integral to growing up.

By the time you're reading this, some new, game-changing tech will have hit the shelves. It is probably powered by AI and promises to replace even more of life's real, human experiences. We'll examine the current state of AI throughout these Habits, and you can always check protectyoungeyes.com and our social media accounts for the latest updates. We'll also share some of our favorite AI experts in appendix 3, "Recommended Tech Resources."

But here's the truth: While technology keeps reinventing itself, the principles that shape healthy digital families do not. These five Habits have stood the test of time. They've been refined through the stories of thousands of parents, hundreds of presentations, grounded in Scripture, backed by science, and lived out in my own home. I promise that when you activate our Five Habits persistently and consistently, you'll see the transformation from scared to prepared, from crazy to calm, and from overwhelmed to confident.

Let's each find the strength and sturdiness required to raise our kids in a healthy, tech-ready family.

Chapter 1

The Experiment None of Us Signed Up For

*Behind every great child is a parent pretty sure they
are screwing it up.*

—Unknown

Most of you reading this book find yourself in the middle of the most heart-filling, energy-sucking, gut-wrenching, emotion-tumbling, love-overflowing role you'll ever have—parenthood.

To state the obvious: Being a parent is more challenging because of technology. Even if you've chosen to have your child wait for a smartphone or social media, every other child seems to be carrying a twelve-foot-deep swimming pool in their pocket in the shape of an iPhone and you're just hoping your own child doesn't fall in and drown. Even though you know in your heart that there's darkness in digital spaces and waiting feels like the right answer, ubiquitous tech makes it tough to take a stand. No one likes the feeling of being the "only one" not engaging with it. This stinks when you're a kid, and it doesn't feel great as a parent either.

So, how do we hold on? What's the secret to swimming upstream in a digital world that's so bent on hooking into as many children as possible? I think the answer starts with understanding what we're saying yes to when we say yes to tech, and this starts with understanding how we got here. After all, the past teaches us about the present. As one history department puts it: "Because history gives us the tools to analyze and explain problems in the past, it positions us to see patterns that might otherwise be invisible in the present—thus providing a crucial perspective for understanding (and solving!) current and future problems."[1]

So, that's where I want to start. As parents, we need knowledge of how we got here, *what* and *who* we're up against, and what we're going to do about it. I've sat across the table from tech executives, and they have very different goals than you do for your child.

Groomed to Worry

My wife and I have an inside joke.

Whenever anything is wrong in the world—whether it's a broken windshield wiper, the next hurricane smashing into Florida, or a son who forgot his saxophone at home *again*, I blame all of it on the same thing.

"You know what caused this, don't you?" she sighs (insert an eye roll).

My response: "It's social media."

I'm *mostly* exaggerating. But what's also true is that even *without* social media, Gen X and millennial parents were destined to be more protective than previous generations of parents because of the things we faced in our own childhoods. The tech revolution is reacting explosively with our own parenting anxieties, for some very specific reasons. This might explain why we are "overprotecting kids in the real world" where they need a lot of free play and autonomy, while "underprotecting them in the virtual world" where they are not developmentally ready for much of what happens to them.[2]

Have you heard the term "latchkey kid"? It goes back to the 1940s, when dads were at war, moms got a job, and kids were on their own and carried a key on a chain around their neck to let themselves into their house after school. But this term became mainstream in the 1980s and early 1990s when both parents were working and kids came home after school to an empty house, where they had to fend for themselves until dinner time.

Sociologists speculate that many of these kids went on to raise their kids in a way that overcompensated for the lack of attention they received from their parents.[3] In this fertile ground, parents who were slightly neglected as kids, ripe to overcorrect how they were parented, became the parents who first raised kids in the digital age.

Thus, we earned our nicknames. While striving for happy, busy, problem-free children of our own, we became "helicopters" (swooping in from time to time to check for danger), "lawnmowers" (blazing a problem-free path for our precious angels), and even "stealth fighters" (those who choose when and where they attack). All too often, issues would hit our radar and strike a nerve: We rushed in rapidly, in force, and often with no warning.

We were attempting to correct what we missed as children. But that impulse goes deeper. As we look back on our early years, we might ask: What if the seeds of today's parenting anxiety were planted long before we became parents?

With the faces we saw on milk jugs, along with *America's Most Wanted*, kids growing up in the '80s and early '90s were left with a lingering feeling that anyone could be kidnapped at *any time*. As we grew older, we watched in horror as the 1999 Columbine school shooting unfolded in front of our eyes. The attack lasted an excruciating fifty minutes, and shocking images and video were quickly shared by the media, gripping the country's attention. Seared in my memory is the image of bloodied seventeen-year-old Patrick Ireland hanging out the window of the school library, reaching for first responders.[4] I will *never* forget it. The events at Columbine had a profound impact on the mindset of young Gen X parents and millennial students. "The definition of normal changed on that day," mourned a parent.[5]

As if we needed more reason to remain vigilant, then came Tuesday, September 11, 2001. Do you remember where you were? I was surrounded by coworkers when the second plane tore into the South Tower—live, in real time. We sat frozen, unable to process the unimaginable scene materializing before our eyes.

It's said that watching the 9/11 attacks unfold live on television deeply traumatized our national psyche. This event marked a shift in the way we interacted with media—the news ticker, or "crawl," permanently appeared at the bottom of the TV screen. According to an article from the *Washington Post*, on 9/11 news networks "dispensed with commercials and reported round-the-clock for days on end. The crawls were an improvisational addition."[6] The 24/7 news cycle adopted in the wake of the 9/11 attacks showed us the same chilling images and videos of the attacks, reinforcing the idea that danger was imminent. *Terrorists could be anywhere.*[7]

Our news would never be the same in this new culture. Like a medieval version of TikTok, the "crawl" kept us hooked as we constantly anticipated that the next bit of news would be the most important story, and many adults couldn't stop watching.[8] Celebrity gossip took a back seat while crisis reporting took over.

All these events combined to change how parents see the world, shifting the dominant mindset toward "the world is dangerous; kids need our constant attention, and we'll do anything to make them happy."[9] Even if you're a younger parent who only remembers 9/11 as an elementary schooler, it doesn't matter—new parental DNA was formed and worked its way into all of us. I was recently reminded that it has also seeped into me.

A few months ago, my thirteen-year-old son was late coming home from a bike ride through our quiet, rural neighborhood. He hadn't taken his Gabb phone, so there were no reassuring pings, no quick texts, and no digital breadcrumbs leading me to him—just silence. As the minutes stretched on, I felt a twinge of worry sneaking in.

Two thoughts hit me in quick succession. The first was almost amusing: *Wait! This must have been what it was like to parent in the 1980s.* Back then, kids vanished on their bikes for hours at a time. Parents generally knew where they were—a park, a neighbor's house, a playground—and they simply trusted the kids would reappear by dinner. No GPS, no "find my iPhone," no constant stream of updates— just faith.

But the second thought wasn't funny at all: *What if the problem isn't him? What if it's me? What if years of tracking apps, bad news headlines, and instant alerts have rewired me to worry?*

Boom. In that moment, I felt the truth: I've been groomed to expect a constant feed of information about my kids and to feel uneasy without these updates. I've grown dependent on a 9/11 ticker tape of their lives scrolling across my mental screen. When this tape stops, anxiety rushes in to fill the gap.

Ironically, my son is a good kid. He knows how to get home. I even knew the general area where he was riding. And, honestly, a phone in his pocket doesn't guarantee his safety. It won't stop a reckless driver or a stranger with bad intentions. Yet the lack of real-time updates still worried me.

That's the challenging balance we wrestle with as parents today: technology as both gift and curse. Yes, I want my son to take a phone next time because the world has changed and there are no pay phones on street corners anymore. But I also need to discipline myself to check his location less and practice being okay with not always knowing. I need to let him be bored and independent sometimes, because those small discomforts are where resilience is born.

If we're serious about raising tech-ready kids, we must be honest about something first: Our own anxieties play a huge role in the choices we make for our kids. We certainly have real reasons to worry, and real reasons to hover—after all, tech can be a tool for safety. Again, do I want my son to take his phone when he takes the next bike ride? You bet. But if we let fear dictate our every move, we'll smother the very strength we're hoping to cultivate in our kids. They can't grow resilient if we don't model resilience ourselves.

So, here's the challenge for me, for you, and for all of us: Let's step back from preconditioned reactions and move toward being proactive, discerning, and wise. If we don't look hard at the *why* behind our tech choices, the very tools we hope will protect our kids may end up undermining the strength we want them to carry into the world.

The Happiness Deception

Not long ago, I was standing in front of 150 school leaders, walking them through our school technology best practices. The room was alive with conversation as I shifted the discussion toward one of the hottest topics in education today: phone-free school policies.

A principal sitting near the front raised her hand. "Chris," she said, "what about Apple Watches? I have a second grader whose anxiety is so intense that her doctor wrote a note allowing her to wear one. That way, her mom can text her during the day and check in."

Her words left me speechless. On the one hand, my heart broke. A child that young should be giggling with friends, enjoying chase games at the playground, and losing herself in crayons and a storybook—not tethered to a device as a lifeline. But at the same time another thought crept in: *Was this really an accommodation for the little girl or for her mom?*

That moment crystallized something for me. Parents, me included, would do almost anything to make our kids' lives safe, happy, and easy. And somewhere along the way, we've been tricked into thinking that short-term comfort equals long-term well-being. But the truth? It doesn't. Sometimes the very thing we think is protecting our kids is quietly making them weaker. So, maybe the real question isn't, *How do we make them happy right now?* Maybe it's, *What will help them flourish tomorrow?* What if happiness, at least the way we define it, was never meant to be the goal at all?

Kathy Shalhoub is an award-winning author and a mom who wrote an excellent piece entitled "My Goal as a Parent Is Not to Make My Kids Happy—It's to See Them Fulfilled." I found myself deeply convicted by her words, especially as a Gen X parent with deep programming from my independent childhood who wants *my* kids to have a different, rejection-free, zero-anxiety, happy childhood.

But that's the problem. As Shalhoub says, "When I focus so intently on creating happy kids, I am implicitly teaching them that any time they're not happy, life is bad. . . . But that only teaches them that a lack of happiness can be fixed with 'stuff' that comes from the outside. *No one has ever found happiness there.*"[10]

And here's the dilemma of the day: iPads, iPhones, YouTube Kids, Instagram, TikTok, and anything with a glowing screen is a joy machine. The promise of a goofy video or another stimulating Blippi adventure will *always* neurologically outgun the backyard or the park. After all, that's what we've trained our kids' brains to crave. But underneath the giggles and scrolling is childhood wonder. This wonder is deep, slow, and innocent. What if it's slipping quietly out of reach? What if we're gaining a kid who's occupied and entertained but losing a future that's secure, confident, and content?

We *do* want kids who are thriving and being all they were created to be. We can raise kids who

- *look up* in awe: love God and admire the divine;
- *reach out* with care: love others and desire their good; and
- *experience wonder*: love life, slowly, suddenly, and serendipitously.

The human heart longs for such things. But it is almost impossible to achieve them looking down, hunched over our devices.[11]

Parents, I know you're not being intentionally malicious when you hand your child an iPhone in the grocery store. When all this started, we were the first parents navigating kids and devices. We often didn't know what we were doing. We believed the marketing, and these things were supposed to make life better. So many of us thought, *My kids seem happy, so what's the big deal?* But the companies behind the screen knew exactly what they were doing. We need to look unflinchingly into the companies that run the internet—Meta, Google, Snapchat, YouTube, TikTok, and Apple—because understanding their motives helps us understand our kids and their digital behavior so much better.

Here lies the path to empathy and understanding. When our kids stumble online, we can readily redirect anger away from them and, instead, point it toward the companies. This also allows us to *expect* our kids to make mistakes (after all, teenagers are *supposed* to screw up). Remember, most of you weren't pitted against PhD data scientists during this unique, curious, impulsive developmental phase of your life. Yes, even though you lived through those pivotal cultural anxieties we just talked about, you didn't have a hundred different people picking a fight with you in your pocket. Your worst moments weren't memorialized, screenshot, shared, and hosted forever on servers. When you consider what your kids are up against, it almost seems silly to get mad at them when they falter online.

The fourteen-year-old version of you would have done the exact same things that your kids might do. And that little head nod of agreement you're doing right now means you're on the correct track, because the path to digital calm and a tech-ready family is paved with warm empathy and deep understanding.

Understanding the Soul of Tech Companies

It's time to admit something uncomfortable: We've been sold a lie.

On January 9, 2007, Steve Jobs stood on the Macworld stage and promised that cramming everything into one pocket-sized device would make humans better. He rolled confidently through a twenty-two-page speech and announced the iPhone—"An iPod, a phone, and an Internet communicator. . . . These are not three separate devices." It was billed as "the Internet in your pocket for the first time ever." The world changed overnight.[12]

And yet—irony alert—Jobs himself kept his children away from these world-changing inventions. When Nick Bilton from the *New York Times* asked in 2010 whether Jobs's kids used the new iPad, Jobs answered, "They haven't used it. We limit the amount of technology our children use at home."[13] Walter Isaacson reported that Jobs family dinners were deliberately tech-free: "Every night Steve insisted on dining at the big kitchen table, talking about books, history and a variety of other things. Nobody ever took out an iPad or a computer. The kids didn't seem addicted to the devices."[14]

So, how did we get from that measured conversation to school districts buying thousands of iPads for classrooms? In 2020, one article began: "[A] school board has unanimously agreed to purchase classroom sets of iPads for all elementary schools in the district" (a total of 3,980 iPads for elementary students and staff).[15] How did we get here? We celebrated convenience and progress—and quietly handed over an enormous new, untested, digital ecosystem of attention-hungry machines to *our children*.

Here's the difficult truth we've been avoiding: These devices weren't designed primarily to make us better; they were designed to capture our attention and monetize it. As comedian-filmmaker Bo Burnham put it, companies don't just want land or products anymore; they want minutes! "They're coming after every minute of your life," he said. "We used to colonize land. That was the thing you could expand into. That's where money was to be made. We colonized the entire earth. There was no other place for businesses and capitalism to expand into and then they realized 'human attention.'"[16] Every idle second is an opportunity to glance and click and to be profiled and targeted.

As parents, we can keep believing the tech-optimism sales pitch, or we can notice what's actually happening and choose differently. Yes, the iPhone was revolutionary—and so were its consequences. Recognizing that truth, especially its implications on children, is the first step toward guiding your family with grace, wisdom, and grit so that it can become tech-ready.

Let's look at social media and its role in monetizing attention.

In March 2025, Sarah Wynn-Williams, former global policy director at Facebook and Meta, published her tell-all book *Careless People*, where she shares intimate details from years with the company's top executives. In April 2025, she appeared before the U.S. Senate Judiciary Committee and answered questions about this very issue. Here's part of that exchange.

> **Senator Marsha Blackburn:** "We've heard that from other whistleblowers that [Meta] were doing research and they knew what was happening, but they were so given to the dollar and having children as the product that they themselves—children were addicted—but, also Facebook and their leadership team had become addicted to the power that they held and to the money that they were making. But talk to me a little bit about your experience with Meta and how they would choose to cover up or deny that they were harming kids."
>
> **Wynn-Williams:** "One example is that Facebook was targeting thirteen-to-seventeen-year-olds—it could identify when they're feeling worthless or helpless or like a failure and they would take that information and share it with advertisers. One of the things about advertising is, advertisers understand that when people don't feel good about themselves it's often a

good time to pitch a product because people are more likely to buy something. And what the company was doing was letting these advertisers know that these thirteen-to-seventeen-year-olds were feeling depressed and saying, 'Now is a really good time to serve them an advertisement,' or if a thirteen-year-old girl would delete her selfie that's a really good time to try and sell her a beauty product."[17]

Another senator asked if the executives at Facebook protected their own children from being exploited like this. Wynn-Williams replied:

Senator, that was one of the things that shocked me when I moved to Silicon Valley is that it's a place full of, you know, wooden Montessori toys. Executives would always speak about how they have no screens in the house. They would say, "Has your teen used the new product we're about to launch?" and [they're] like, "My teenager isn't allowed on Facebook, I don't allow my teenager Instagram." These executives know. They know the harm that this product does. They don't allow their own teenagers to use the products that Meta develops. I mean, the hypocrisy is at every level.[18]

Somehow, we've managed to turn reality upside down. Parents, pastors, and principals remain trapped in the techno-utopian glow of the early 2000s, when every new gadget and platform was hailed as "progress." But that dream has soured. Two decades later, piles of evidence are becoming mountains—patterns of corporate behavior that tell a far darker story about what technology is doing to our schools, our children, and our culture. And yet the people with the power to respond—the ones who could stem the tide—continue to look away. Worse, they face no consequences for their inaction, even though measurable data tells us something is very wrong.

I received the following message through our website from a father named Brandon. "Dear Protect Young Eyes Team, I'm a data scientist. I think you might benefit from our FBI Violent Crimes Against Children data. I've written a program that can analyze 9,000+ FBI press releases for trends in apps." I was floored to see Brandon's work. Thanks to it, we have a unique FBI dataset of 9,441 press releases related to violent crimes against children.[19] This means we have eye-opening data showing us the role that technology plays in exploitation—and this is not just data. Each press release points to a real event that happened to a real child, with a real perpetrator who often made contact online. The numbers Brandon assembled shine a spotlight on patterns that every parent needs to see. For example, predators don't target all children the same way. For the very young, the crimes most often involve the creation or exchange of child sexual abuse material (also referred to as child pornography), which piques their natural curiosities. But once children reach the age where smartphones and social media become common, the crimes shift toward enticement, coercion, and sex trafficking—crimes built on *communication, manipulation, and access.*

Here's what the FBI dataset shows:

Victim Age	Most Frequent Crime
2–7	Distribution or Receipt of Child Pornography
8	Production of Child Pornography
9–15	Enticement
16–17	Sex Trafficking

Think about that. Once a child enters the tween and early teen years, social media becomes more common, and they are immersed in apps like TikTok or Snapchat. That means grooming. "Enticement." Manipulation. Exploitation. Predators aren't just watching from the shadows; they're able to chat, like, and follow. Let me foreshadow Habit 4: Delaying addictive technologies matters. Every year you hold back access to addictive social media platforms, while strengthening your digital trust, gives your child's brain time to grow stronger before facing the relentless pull of enticement.

What's more, not all apps are created equal. Out of the more than nine thousand FBI press releases analyzed, fifty-five different platforms were linked to crimes against children. Some stood out far more than others. For example, Snapchat dominated in enticement and sextortion cases. Its disappearing-photo feature lowers inhibitions, making kids feel safer sending images that vanish.

Crime Type	#1 App	Other Common Apps
Enticement	Snapchat	Kik, Instagram, X (Twitter)
Sex Trafficking	X (Twitter)	Kik, Snapchat, Instagram, Discord
Online Exploitation	Kik	Instagram, Snapchat, TikTok

These are not neutral spaces. Instead, they are the digital equivalent of leaving your child alone in a crowded city at midnight. Consequently, parents must know where digital problems perpetuate—and teach their kids to recognize the traps (or avoid these spaces altogether; #delayistheway).

According to Hany Farid, a professor at the University of California and the developer of PhotoDNA, "We don't treat the harms from technology the same way we treat the harms of romaine lettuce. One person dies, and we pull every single head of romaine lettuce out of every store," yet the children's exploitation problem is decades old. "Why do we not have spectacular technologies to protect kids online?"[20]

The answer: There's no incentive to create them. Here's why.

Understanding the Limits of Internet Law

Did you know there's a golden loophole in US law that lets tech companies turn a blind eye while our kids are being harmed online? It's called Section 230, and it was created by Congress in 1996 when the internet was still brand new. In what's sometimes referred to as "the twenty-six words that built the modern internet," lawmakers wanted to give tech companies freedom to grow without fear of lawsuits. They never imagined how this law would be twisted. Instead of protecting families, it's now a powerful shield that allows companies to avoid responsibility, even when their platforms are used for:

- child sexual abuse material (CSAM, also referred to as "child pornography" in law)
- grooming and sextortion networks
- sex trafficking
- revenge pornography, stalking, and domestic abuse[21]

Sworn testimony shows that media platforms know this is happening, but Section 230 gives them cover to say, *"Not our problem."* Countless families have pleaded for harmful content, especially CSAM, to be taken down. Law enforcement asks for cooperation. But companies point to these twenty-six words constantly and say they don't have to help:

> No provider or user of an interactive computer service shall be treated as the publisher or speaker of any information provided by another information content provider.[22]

Right now, many companies are using this argument to win and escape accountability in US courts.[23]

Congressman Chris Cox, one of the original authors of Section 230, once said that its goal was "to help clean up the Internet, not to facilitate people doing bad things on the Internet."[24] Instead, it is being wielded as a judicial weapon, enabling predators while silencing victims.

Maybe you've never had an interest in internet law—I get it. But maybe you're starting to realize how this silent weapon is being used to perpetuate harm and suffering for families. Here's the hard truth: The companies aren't coming to protect our kids. Incentives drive corporate behavior, and there's no incentive for them to change course. The government isn't stepping in. The courts are complicit and standing by. That means it's up to us—parents, families, and communities—to be highly motivated to take matters into our own hands, understand what we're up against, and fight like crazy for change.

Consider the following stories.

A young teenage boy was manipulated on Snapchat by someone posing as a teen girl. He and his friend were tricked into creating sexual abuse material. Their abuser uploaded the footage to X (formerly Twitter), where it was viewed over 200,000 times.

The boy and his mother begged X to remove it. They submitted a government-issued ID to prove he was a minor. X responded that the content did not violate its community standards. The platform continued to profit from views and engagement as this child's trauma was consumed by hundreds of thousands.[25]

When sued, X argued that *even if it was working with sex traffickers*, it was immune from liability under Section 230. Thus far, the courts have agreed with X. As of this writing, the case is on appeal in the Ninth Circuit.

Another example concerns Snapchat, which is widely used to distribute drugs. It has successfully deflected any financial or legal responsibility for hundreds of fentanyl deaths that could have easily been prevented.[26]

A further, devastating example was the grooming of a thirteen-year-old boy on Roblox—a platform that built its business model on targeting kids under thirteen.[27] With over 110 million daily active users,[28] 40 percent of whom are under age thirteen, it has become a playground for predators.[29] The teen's abuse moved from Roblox to Snapchat and eventually to X, where the predator bragged about what he was doing and posted publicly about his plan to kidnap the boy. He followed through, abducting the child across state lines. Users alerted

X and local law enforcement, but X refused to help. The boy was only rescued because a gas station attendant noticed something was off and intervened.[30]

Imagine a world where anyone with a bit of coding knowledge (or skills with ChatGPT) can build a digital gateway that connects children to adults—no barriers and no oversight. An app appears in Apple's App Store with nothing more than a self-assigned age rating. Children step inside via a single tap, and harm becomes possible—and even encrypted. The cycle repeats, dismissed in court every time. This is not some cautionary tale; it's the reality we are living in now.

It's hardly surprising, then, that industry leaders like Steve Jobs and Bill Gates, the architects of our digital age, quietly kept their own children at arm's length from the same technologies they gifted to the world.[31]

Their stance was never about rejecting technology. In a twist of irony, it echoed a deeper wisdom that we at Protect Young Eyes have trumpeted for years: the right child, the right tool, at the right time. Why? Because childhood is fragile, a fleeting season of development that shapes who we become. Yet during these years, instead of following the majority who say yes to smartphones and social media, perhaps we should pause. Maybe we should listen to the quiet minority. They're the 5 percent who say "slow" or even (rightfully) "no."

Strikingly, that minority is not made up of anti-tech skeptics on the sidelines. It includes the very people who invented these technologies in the first place.

Understanding Our Kids' Need to Attach

We can't find digital calm unless we understand what's causing the chaos. When we appreciate how important historical factors might influence our parenting and honestly assess the power and motivations of the companies we're up against, we are empowered to adjust.

Now let's level up our understanding of why our *kids* do certain things. They are uniquely wired to be drawn to us and the physical (and digital) world around them. As you'll see, whether they're four months old, four years old, or a teenager, interfering with their inherent desire to attach and connect can send them spinning.

This all starts at infancy.

I recently had a conversation with Dr. Stacy Drury, psychiatrist-in-chief at Boston Children's Hospital. In her own words, she is "obsessed with babies" and loves watching parents interact with them because babies are "this incredible ball of potential and joy." Looking back, can't you envision seeing such dynamic promise in your own little one?

"Early connections with a safe, responsive, and aware caregiver shape the brain," Dr. Drury told me. "They shape your physiological responses. They shape your immune system. And they shape your capacity to understand and interact with the world *for the rest of your life.*"

In 2014, Dr. Drury tested a provocative new theory: If children bond closely with a parent in the first year of life, this leaves lasting genetic protection, potentially shielding them from disease risks. Her findings were astonishing. She was the first scientist to show that *extreme stress in infancy can biologically age a child* by shortening the tips of chromosomes (known as telomeres). Shorter telomeres are linked to higher risks for heart disease, cognitive decline, diabetes, and mental illness in adults.[32]

Attach with your child now and improve their health as adults later—remarkable!

Furthermore, proper attachment starts at the very beginning. Doctors still don't fully understand some of the things that happen during and after childbirth. One of those is the beneficial influence of skin-to-skin contact: It calms and relaxes both mother and baby; regulates the baby's heart rate and breathing, helping them to better adapt to life outside the womb; stimulates digestion and an interest in feeding; and so much more.[33] Little humans (and their mothers and fathers) desperately need skin-to-skin contact with other humans to feel cared for, safe, and connected. Isn't that amazing?

In the Bible, *The Message* translation of Psalm 139:13–16 gives us a vivid explanation of how we are shaped by outside forces:

> Oh yes, you shaped me first inside, then out;
> you formed me in my mother's womb.
> I thank you, High God—you're breathtaking!
> Body and soul, I am marvelously made!
> I worship in adoration—what a creation!
> You know me inside and out,
> you know every bone in my body;
> You know exactly how I was made, bit by bit,
> how I was sculpted from nothing into something.
> Like an open book, you watched me grow from
> conception to birth;
> all the stages of my life were spread out before you,
> The days of my life all prepared
> before I'd even lived one day.

I love the phrases "you shaped me first inside, then out" and "how I was sculpted from nothing into something." This passage reminds us that we are shaped by divine forces *and* by the people around us—even if we remember none of it.

Infants rely on nonverbal cues like facial expressions, tone, and eye contact to feel secure.[34] When a parent's attention is repeatedly divided by their digital device, the infant may begin to associate the device they're looking at with emotional neglect. The concept of *technoference* addresses how modern technology alters attachment dynamics. Parents' constant phone use interrupts the natural rhythm of bonding.[35] This confusion can affect identity formation and relational security.

Consider for a moment a parent who is constantly filming their child with their phone. Based on our knowledge of children and attachment, even these well-meaning behaviors might disrupt attunement. Therapist Catherine Knibbs comments, "I wonder how infants/toddlers make sense of a thing (portable device) that is pointed at them, that is in so many interactions whilst the holder of 'the thing' coos, 'Smile'?"[36]

Something Dr. Stacy Drury told me blew my mind:

> I am most anxious about the one-year-old reaching for the phone, and the reason they are reaching for the phone is not necessarily that they want the phone. But because the phone is taking Mom's attention away, and so the baby is saying, "I want that because I want my mom's attention on me." Parents completely misinterpret this, and they'll give them the phone and then the kid will kind of stare at it trying to understand why this is more important than me. They don't have the words, but they inherently know they want Mom, and this thing is in the way.

That is a powerful example! Dr. Drury went on to share this shocking statement: "The only thing I know stronger than heroin are babies. So, when you are paying attention to a phone, you're missing all the things that make being a parent survivable. You don't get the joys of quiet moments and those precious smiles or those times when peek-aboo was like the best thing ever. We need those as much as they do."

Here's where I need to stomp out some shame, because none of us is perfect. According to Dr. Drury, "Having a non-responsive parent is not a problem if it occurs in short doses. However, if it occurs over longer periods, experts have significant concerns about the detrimental impacts on a baby's development." So, we can start right now to develop a conscious habit of responsiveness despite our devices.

Understanding Our Kids' Need to Connect

"Attachment is the most critical component of human development," remarked Dr. Jim Winston, a clinical psychologist and friend with over thirty years of experience, in one of our conversations. He went on to add, "After the first couple of years of life, *adolescence* is the second most critical time in brain development. This is when they need to *connect* with those around them."

Maybe that's why teens can be such a mystery to us, especially as they change.

Dr. Lisa Damour is well known for her level, research-based approach to raising teens, an age period she has studied her entire thirty-plus years as a clinical psychologist. On her *Ask Lisa* podcast she entreats parents to not be offended when our tweens and teens don't want to spend time with us. "As they loosen ties to us, which is their job, *they should be strengthening ties* to other people [friends]," she explains.[37]

Dr. Damour went on to share this golden phrase: It's not personal. "None of this is personal. If I had to come up with a title for a book about parenting teenagers, it would be *It's Not Personal*. It's kind of stunning, but the job of teenagers is to become independent, right? . . . And that's why it's not personal. The kid is getting ready to go, and the only way they can get ready to go is if they sort of loosen ties and become more private."[38]

Let's get one thing straight: Our teens still need us. They may tower over us, talk like adults, and roll their eyes like pros, but don't mistake this distance for disinterest. Don't throw in the towel after one brushoff, one sarcastic jab, or one shunned attempt at engaging your small talk. This is when it matters most—they're learning how to love, how to trust, and how to belong.

And just as our teens are testing their relational limits with us, in slips social media, a digital siren offering connection through pings, posts, and perfectly sublime AI companions. These omnipresent, human-sounding chatbots and apps promise friendship on demand— but they also drag in a toxic entourage: manipulation, algorithms, predators, exploitation, data breaches, and a bottomless scroll of distraction.

I desperately want parents to understand that, deep down, the reasons kids want tech and AI companions and social media are pure and expected. *Give me my friends.*

The fourteen-year-old version of each of us would also have begged for these apps. But this modern technology is like sugar in the food pyramid—quick energy but not sustaining.

It mimics nutrition without providing it.

It pretends to be God without the divine.

It deceives by feigning connection without nurturing it.

It drips quick-hit dopamine without cultivating lasting wonder.

Here is more of Dr. Winston's insight from our conversation: "The teenage years are when the need for social connection is as powerful an instinct as hunger. Some kids are incapable of managing the digital overstimulation. Social media companies know this and have weaponized it. They exploit this vulnerability to keep kids glued to their screens and apps."

How do we fight back? With what's real. Face to face, eye to eye, and heart to heart. This is the kind of visceral connection our ancient human brains are wired for from cradle to college and from baby giggles to teenage sighs. That includes your tween's brain, your teen's brain, and every version in between.

If you've stepped back from your teen because they seem to want nothing to do with you, take a breath. This isn't about guilt or shame. If screens have filled more hours than you'd like, you're not a bad parent. Receive grace upon grace. No perfect parenting is required to keep things going—just presence, patience, and a willingness to try again.

So, we're going to continue this journey as a cohort of flawed parents and caregivers. It's worth noting that throughout these pages, I will frequently use the term *parents*. That's not meant to feel exclusionary, but it's a simple way to refer to a wide group of awesome humans: caregivers, foster parents, adoptive parents, and grandparents. You have young humans in your life whom you love a great deal, and they spend time in digital spaces. That's you I'm talking to. You are who this book is written for! You *can* find digital calm.

Now that you know more about yourself, the tech, and your kid, let's dig into the five key Habits of the tech-ready family. The first one starts with relationship—your child's connection to *you*—because that caring relationship is the foundation of everything you do for them online and offline.

5 Takeaways for Parents

1. **Short-term happiness vs. long-term fulfillment:** modern parenting often prioritizes keeping children immediately content, especially through technology, but this may undermine their development of resilience, creativity, and emotional health.

2. **Technology as both a comfort and a trap:** Digital devices easily occupy and please children, but they rarely build the deep relational, emotional, and character strengths that truly prepare kids for life.

3. **Shifting blame from kids to tech companies:** By understanding the manipulative designs of tech platforms, we can shift frustration away from our children's mistakes and focus on guiding them with empathy, recognizing the unprecedented digital pressures that today's youth face.

4. **Technology's true business model:** Modern digital platforms aren't selling products to users but are extracting users' attention and data to sell to advertisers, especially by targeting vulnerable groups like teens when their spirits feel low.

5. **Attachment and connection are essential to thriving:** Constant device use can interfere with child-parent bonding from the newborn phase to the teen years. Kids need present, responsive adults.

"Do Just Two Things This Week" Checklist

☐ Do a digital anxiety self-assessment, with scores ranging from one to five. One means you're chill and five means you're concerned about everything (some of which even keeps you up at night). How does that anxiety affect you, your decisions, and your relationship with your kids?

☐ Write down all your digital concerns. Then go in your bedroom or bathroom, look in the mirror, and say the items in your list out loud, one at a time. Pause after each item and say, "I'm not going to freak out!" We'll find a way through them together in the Five Habits.

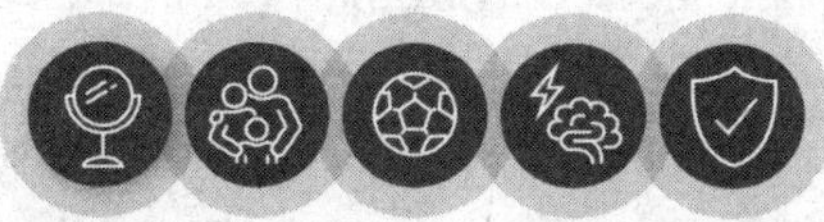

Chapter 2

Habit 1: Model the Right Behaviors

Don't worry that your children never listen to you.
Worry that they are always watching you.

—Robert Fulghum

On a recent speaking trip to Nashville, I got to the airport and did something I had never done before, even though I've given more than eight hundred presentations.

I forgot to bring my phone.

I realized it just after passing the TSA guy as I was checking my pockets for things to put in the bin for security. Panic came over me as I checked my watch, realizing that I had about a 5 percent chance of getting home and back to the airport in time for my flight. And missing the flight had a 95 percent chance of causing me to be late for my speaking engagement that evening.

I decided to try the two-day trip phone-free. I was confident it was the correct decision, *but the initial anxiety I felt was overwhelming.* I was convinced that I had just doomed myself to an unimaginable hardship.

My first obstacle was not having a boarding pass. No problem, because I had my driver's license as the required ID, so the gate agent printed me a paper version—first crisis averted. We boarded the plane shortly afterward, and I found my seat. Normally, this is when I would quickly check email, social media, and texts upon boarding a flight to ensure that I've caught up with everything important before enabling the dreaded airplane mode, cutting me off from most communication. But I could not do it this time. In fact, I didn't even feel any compulsion to check my phone. I just sat there and looked out the window and wondered what it would be like to be a worker on the tarmac dodging big airplanes all day like the frogs in *Frogger*.

Next, the flight attendant gave her usual instructions about safety and seatbelts. For the first time in years, I knew where the exits were on my plane! I even smiled at her while she spoke, since I was perhaps the only person looking at her.

The initial anxiety that I felt in the airport was slowly dissipating.

I arrived in Nashville, took a screenshot of Google Maps on my MacBook, and kept it open in the passenger seat of my rental car, so I knew where to meet friends for lunch.

I had the best experience of my trip when I got to the hotel. My Hilton app normally reminds me with persistence to use "contactless check-in" so I can go right to my room. I'll concede that this option is sometimes nice after a long trip, but I couldn't choose it this time. I had to talk to Markus at the front desk so I could get my key card. In that moment, Markus asked me the strangest question: "Would you like to rent a betta fish for the night? His name is Steven."

The hotel was doing a fundraiser for a local charity and had two small fish tanks. For an additional ten dollars, people staying at the hotel could "rent a pet" for the night. Amazing! It was a serendipitous encounter (both with Markus and Steven the betta) that only took place *because* I forgot my phone. And what about the eighty-five-year-old retiree named Howard working part-time as the breakfast host the next day? With no phone to distract me, I said hello to him. He then sat at my table, sharing his adventures from years ago as a truck driver in Green Bay, Wisconsin. One particularly memorable night during a blizzard, his rig froze and he had to spend the night at a diner where the waitress was hungover and had a black eye because she had fallen off a bull she rode the night before. What a gem! I got to experience this marvelous story!

All this happened because I forgot my phone.

My gosh. When was the last time you considered the richness of the world around us? And how often do our children watch us embracing the power of *human* connection instead of constantly being *connected*? Over the course of two days, I realized how blessed it felt to be phone-free and how important it was for my children to observe me being more phone-free around them! I realized I hadn't been modeling this very well. And if I don't model this, how will they see it in action?

———

Let me take you back to some OG parenting advice from the Bible; it has a lot to do with modeling what we want our children to repeat. Immediately after Moses recounted the Ten Commandments, he gave the Hebrews powerful instructions from God about raising children before they headed into the promised land:

> You shall love the LORD your God with all your heart and with all your soul and with all your might. And these words that I command you today shall be on your heart. You shall teach them diligently to your children, and shall talk of them when you sit in your house, and when you walk by the way, and when you lie down, and when you rise. You shall bind them as a sign on your hand, and they shall be as frontlets between your eyes. You shall write them on the doorposts of your house and on your gates. (Deuteronomy 6:5–9)

The *repetition* and *modeling* stand out to me in these verses. If you want your children to remember something during this unique developmental stage, do this thing over and over with them. Show them! Tell them! As we often say in our live presentations, "Say it so often that they're rolling their eyes and finishing your sentences." God knew that repetition and modeling work in our children.

If we fail to step in with guidance, Dr. YouTube, Dr. TikTok, and Dr. ChatGPT will take our place—and their office hours run 24/7. These platforms operate on a principle that Scripture has taught for centuries: Formation happens through repetition and example. Here is the pressing question: Are we more faithful and consistent in shaping our children toward what is good, excellent, and kind than the algorithms shaping them otherwise?

When you're repeating and modeling your values to your children, you don't have to be perfect, elegant, deep, or articulate. Instead, aim for being consistent, quick, curious, and caring.

It starts with *us*.

Bottom line: Would you want your children to use their technology just like you do? Should they imitate where you use it, how you use it, and what you use it for? Would you want them to have the same relationship with screen time as you do?

If you're wondering how we define "screen time," I'm glad, because it's complicated. Does watching the smart TV count as screen time? Partially, but mostly no. One way to see a difference is between screen time where we "lean back" (going to the movies or watching a movie at home together) versus where we "lean forward" (hunched over playing *Brawl Stars* on the iPad).[1]

Many organizations have published guidelines related to children and screen time. Although each study has different nuances, there are common themes:

- Almost zero screen time of any kind is recommended for our littlest littles, ages 0–2 (Dr. Stacy Drury told me she sticks with age 3, keeping those first 1,000 days of life as interference-free as possible).[2] If babies or young children are using a screen, stick with co-watched educational programming and video calls.

- Whatever amount of screen time your kids have right now, less isn't going to hurt them. There aren't any studies showing harmful childhood effects from lower levels of screen time (in fact, it's almost always the opposite[3]).
- *Technoference* is real and is an emerging issue. Adult technology use shapes parent/child relationships and forms a child's perception of tech use.[4]

Each of these points is important, but the last bullet is what we're focusing on when we talk about modeling.

I want to repeat something here. *You're not a bad parent if you pick up your phone.* After all, the emails, sports schedules, and reminders are entangled in parenthood like genetics. And so, I want you to hear once more that this chapter seeks to encourage us to be more *mindful*. Not *shame-filled*. None of us is at our best when we're full of shame. Receive abundant grace. Cultivate abundant mindfulness. This discussion is full of both actions.

I must repeat this because whenever I share thoughts about parents putting devices down, I'm met with strong opinions. In a podcast interview, I shared a story about a parent who often took her young daughter to the park.[5] Her daughter would play, swing, and slide while Mom sat on the bench, often scrolling on her phone. One day, this mom decided to put the phone down and simply enjoy nature and watch her daughter play, and something unexpected happened. While playing, her daughter would periodically look at mom—just a cute little glance. Mom loved those glances but also realized she had been missing them while scrolling.

After sharing this story in a social media post, I received intense reactions from both sides. Some took it as encouragement to be more present. Others reacted with fiery responses about being shamed and declared that I "must be a dad who never takes care of the kids." I never intended to make anyone feel bad about looking at a phone. Instead, I was encouraging us to be mindful so that the phone doesn't constantly rob us of those *human* experiences—such as a simple, cute, over-the-shoulder glance from a daughter. If we're not careful, could our screen habits have even more significant impacts on our children?

One article published just before the pandemic garnered significant attention because of its title: "Communications Time Bomb: Parents' Smartphone Use Could Be the New Secondhand Smoke."[6] Now, that's clickable. But is it factual?

There are obvious differences between nicotine and technology. One enters your bloodstream and has a physiological influence. The other is behavioral and obviously doesn't cross the blood/brain barrier. Even if the title is a bit sensationalized, I get what the writer is saying because both interfere with the thriving of our children. The writer, a speech-language pathologist, goes on to say:

> When parents or caregivers spend too much time turning away from their kids and toward technology, the foundation for a child's communication skills is weakened. In a world with competing priorities and limited time, experts in my field of speech and language development are already seeing the impacts on children who have missed out on hours of essential, real-life face time—and the results are concerning. Many of my colleagues across the nation say they are seeing more children entering kindergarten with limited communication and social skills. Older children, they say, are unable to handle formal social interactions, like ordering from waitstaff at a restaurant.[7]

Maybe you're saying to yourself, "Okay, Chris, I get it. I need to show them how. But I'm kind of addicted. So, give me some super practical steps because I don't have time for full-on, cold-turkey therapy here." Let's start with an easy one.

Post with Their Permission

I remember a conversation years ago with a friend who first introduced me to the idea of digital consent from our children.

In the age of deepfake technology and nudifying applications (both driven by AI), it's more critical than ever for our children, and especially our teens, to understand the value of digital media. Every picture and video of everyone is valuable and can be used for good or life-changing harm. So, if we want our kids to respect digital photos of friends that might get passed around, we can use moments where we capture pictures of them as teaching moments. We can show our kids the photo we've taken, disclose whom we're going to send it to, and ask for their approval. We can also give them a quick reminder about the significance of pictures among their friends and the need to treat pictures with care.

In doing this, we start to realize how much personal information about our family we share with a lot of people we only "kind of" know. This is often most true with significant milestones such as first days of school, birthdays, and holidays. With our phones in hand, we can't tap and capture enough of their cute moments, and we can't wait to share them with others. But name, general age, birthday, location, and school are gold to identity thieves and predators.[8] And if this information can be figured out from posts, what's to stop such people?

Bottom line: As caregivers, keep your shares with non-close family infrequent, discrete, and careful. Ensure that close family members know your expectations with the photos you do share, which might prevent Grandma from also oversharing on Facebook. That said, there's a version of "oversharing" that can actually *help* our kids.

Announce Your Tech Intentions

Dr. Rebecca Winthrop is a global education expert who understands teen thriving. During a conversation at the World Economic Forum, she told me that narrating the *what* and *why* of things you're doing during the day to your teens is like a cuddle to them. They might not tell you, but they like it.

As parents, we're going to use our phones around our kids. We sometimes *have* to. And when we do, consider giving them a *mini play-by-play*. Narrate what you're doing online when you're with them. It might look like, "Hey, I need to take this call, but I'll be right back with you," or "I need to check the school website to see what your schedule is, but then you'll have my full attention again."

This small change does a couple of things. First, it shows our kids that there are good uses of technology. Second, it's a great accountability tool for us so that after we do the thing we announced, we don't pivot to social media, where we can easily lose another fifteen minutes (minimum, right?). And, third, if we announced we'd be done after the call or text and they see us stay on the phone, you can be sure they'll remind you. It's great accountability! What kid doesn't love an opportunity to call out their parents? When we remember that they're constantly watching, even doing nothing at all can show them a better way to be present.

Show Them How to Do Nothing

The Italians have a saying, "*il dolce far niente*," which means "the sweetness of doing nothing." According to a professor of public health, "It's not laziness. It's presence. It's choosing, for once, *not* to rush."[9]

An article written by Ephrat Livni opens by saying, "Busy people don't have epiphanies. Great realizations occur when we're chilling—staring up at the sky, out at the sea, or wandering among trees."[10] Haven't you found that to be true? The world might not have $E = mc^2$ if Einstein hadn't been inclined to sail aimlessly and toss rocks, seemingly without purpose.

Although we often focus on kid screen time, parental attention has also been eviscerated by curated feeds and algorithms. Our brains are no match for today's tech, and our adult attention span is quickly becoming endangered. All the while, our children are continuing to watch us closely.

Neuroscientist Alicia Walf says it's critical for brain health to let yourself be bored from time to time. Your brain gets a much-needed rest when you're not working it too hard.[11] In those moments that might seem empty and needless, strategies and solutions that have been there all along in their embryonic forms are given space and come to life. For example, my executive coach once asked me to take a call while walking in our neighborhood instead of standing at my desk on a Zoom call, because he knows movement in nature can shake a few new things loose in our minds. Have you also noticed this?

Famous writers have said that their most creative ideas come to them when they're moving furniture, taking a shower, or pulling weeds.[12] These eureka moments are called *insight*.

In the Bible, we read that when Mary miraculously learned she was expecting baby Jesus, she "treasured up all these things, pondering them in her heart." (Luke 2:19). *Pondering* isn't a Google search. It isn't searching for a YouTube video or asking ChatGPT for answers. It's weighing meaning carefully with your own inspired thoughts and mental wanderings, letting ideas simmer. Believers in God also allow his Spirit to wander in and nudge their thoughts.

Even though it has been more than eighteen years, I can still point to the spot on the sidewalk during a long run where I knew I had to admit my struggle with addiction and decided to come clean. I also still know where I was walking in downtown Grand Rapids when I realized it was time to quit my consulting job and pursue a completely different path working in junior high ministry.[13]

Experiencing moments of "nothing," often while strolling quietly or enjoying a run, completely redirected my life toward "something" much better. What about you?

Parents, do your children observe you leaving space in your life to just toss or kick rocks? How can you show your kids "the sweetness of doing nothing" in the digital age? It doesn't have to be radical—it can be micro-moves. Here are a few:

1. No digital devices in the bathroom. (I shudder to think about the germs on our devices.)
2. Ditch phone holders in your car—especially if you're the kid chauffeur.
3. Don't take your phone if you just need to get gas. Or a gallon of milk. If you're concerned about safety, put it in the glove box.
4. No, you don't need to check email at the stoplight!
5. Use the grocery checkout line with a human, and don't check your phone. Talk to the teen ringing you up, who might really need your smile!
6. If you fly, try traveling without AirPods. The person next to you might give *you* an epiphany.
7. No phones in bedrooms. It's good for kids and parents. Or, if you must, at least don't keep the phone on the nightstand next to your head—place it across the room.
8. Be more aware of how often you take photos of your child with a smartphone. Try just enjoying them and absorbing what they're doing. This might actually be more memorable.
9. Never use your phones at meals—make dinner a raucous, relational event. Trust me; in a few years, you'll *long* for more meals with your graduated kiddos.
10. Don't use your phone at appointments (dentists, doctors, etc.). Talk to people. Connect with your kids. Read a magazine. Ponder life.
11. (I know this one will be tough for many.) If safe, go low-tech while exercising. For example, we live in the country, and I don't run with a phone or earbuds. I just have an expired license in my pocket and a metal ID tag velcroed to my left shoe. I always let my wife know where I'm going. (But

many may find this a safety issue, so consider setting your phone on "Do Not Disturb" while out for a run or walking the dog.)

I promise you, embracing even a few of these recommendations will bring you a surprising sense of calm and rub off on your kids. It's a win-win. Doing a few of these together draws your kids in and creates a shared sense of what's important to your family. Then consider writing down the values you care most about.

Establish Your Family's Values

Businesses create core values that shape corporate culture, behaviors, and decisions. One company I worked for started most meetings by having attendees repeat the company's values, and I still remember them many years later:

- Honor God
- Optimism
- Passion for excellence
- Service to others

(It also made the acronym H.O.P.S., which beer-loving coworkers enthusiastically embraced!)

And sometimes a decision was made simply because it was the one that lined up best with the company's core values. These words influenced how we hired, led our teams, and behaved.

The same can be true in our families. Our behaviors flow out of what we value. But how often do parents and children have open conversations about our values? Identifying what matters most to your family is important: It helps you determine how to make decisions, what to say yes and no to, and shapes your family's relationship with technology. We'll talk about making a list of tech rules next (what I call a family media plan). But those rules will need to line up with your family's values to be workable. So, that's where we'll start!

Mell and Joe Hashey from Strong Family Co have shared their process for developing family values.[14] Their approach is calm and simple. Mell points out that you don't have to make it a big to-do. Start by having a conversation with your partner about what is important to your family. Mell and her husband, Joe, set out to discover what really mattered to their family, establishing five to seven core family values.

For two weeks, Mell and Joe separately wrote down everything that was valuable to them—from small things to big things. They ended up with a long list including reading, adventure, playfulness, gratitude—anything that occurred to them individually in those couple of weeks.

Next, they came together for a meeting and went through their lists with a practice called "Kill, Keep, or Combine." They determined that some items on the list weren't that important, so they "killed" them. They kept some others and combined similar items.

Mell and Joe continued to have these deep conversations until they ended up with a list of five to seven items. After they established these family values, they had a meeting with the kids to communicate what the values were and what they meant. Joe and Mell then posted the values in their home but took them less as rules than as openers for conversations with the children, putting those values into play in real-life scenarios.

Once you clearly identify your values, the rest starts to fall into place. These values become your filter for how you make decisions about tech and about life offline. Figuring out your home's "tech rules" suddenly feels less overwhelming, because one naturally flows from the other. And when it's time to enforce those rules, those shared values act like an invisible authority figure in the room who is steady and respected by everyone. This isn't about control, but rather clarity. And now with that foundation in place, it's time to put it into practice by creating your family media plan.

Create a Family Media Plan

After your family's values are in place, it's time to decide how to apply them to digital spaces with a family media plan.

What is this plan? It contains the basic rules for how *everyone* in your family uses technology. Think of it as your family's digital code of conduct that everyone abides by. Yes, that means parents are also included in this! I want you to lead by example and follow the rules you're asking your kids to follow.

I want your kids to also be part of this process. Plan it out before explaining it to them. List the who, what, when, where, and how long for using technology (I'll give you some examples soon). You have the final say, but let your kids influence some of the decisions by giving their suggestions.

What Does a Family Media Plan Look Like?

Your plan can look however you want. Don't get too caught up in its form—I've seen multiple variations ranging from a fully designed poster to bullets on a list. Here are questions to consider:

- What values are important to our family? (List the family values you just figured out earlier.)
- Who needs to be around while using tech? (e.g., siblings, caregivers, mom or dad, grandparents, other family members)
- What tech is each person allowed to use? (e.g., tablet, Dad's phone, Mom's phone, Chromebook, gaming console, home computer)
- When can tech be used? (e.g., before bedtime, on weekends, when guests are over, before and/or after dinner, before and/or after school, before and/or after homework)
- (For kids) When do I need to ask permission to use the tech? (e.g., using a device, playing games, watching videos, downloading new apps, watching shows/movies)

- Where can we use tech? (e.g., car, school, church, in public, bedroom, bathroom, friend's house, grandparents' house)
- How long can we use tech?

Remember: These bullets also apply to parents! These are for *the family*. For example, if parents know the passcodes for kids' phones, then spouses know the passcodes for each other's phones.

In appendix 3, you'll find a printable form you can use with your family. But you can also do what one brilliant mom did. After attending one of our live presentations, she bulleted out a few key notes on a piece of paper that she put in the drawer where most technology was plugged in. She included ideas like:

- Ask permission.
- Every device is on loan.
- Co-play
- Curiosity
- Walk away.
- Mom and Dad are safe.
- Help create the rules.
- Report ads.
- If you get mad when I take it away, it's gone for a day.
- Am I going to be helpful or hurtful?

All these things are straight from our talk! You'll find out more about them during this journey through the Habits. This simple piece of paper served as a regular reminder of the most important tech rules in the home every time a family member reached in the drawer for a device. This makes me think that Moses was referring to something similar in Deuteronomy 6:5–9 with its repetition and constant reminders. Whether this mom realized it or not, that simple piece of paper was quietly creating a foundation she could build on.

Clarity Can Lead to Trust

Without a family media plan, parental anxiety is often higher because you might be tempted to check devices all the time. If your kids are constantly surprised by your checking, you might erode trust by giving them the impression that they are constantly untrustworthy. Here's a conversation I had with a mom who felt herself slipping into that very situation:

> **Mom:** "My problem now is [my daughter] thinks I'm too restrictive. Our cutoff time on the phone is at 10 p.m. But recently she's been spending so much more time on Pinterest that it's worrying me—like sometimes two hours. I am so anxious. I always look at her screen time and monitor it, and this gives me anxiety. But she gets mad if I question her. She's fourteen. And some people say to let go of some control so that our relationship isn't too fragile, 'cuz it is now."
>
> **Me:** "You'll have to decide. It sounds like you're assuming that she's making poor choices on Pinterest with this extra time. And although I don't know if that's true or not, I bet she can sense that you don't approve. In other words, what you've described sounds like a 'you versus your daughter' situation and not a 'you with your daughter' situation. I'm wondering if you are the one who might need to change first."
>
> **Mom:** "Yes, this is a good point. . . . It is definitely a 'me versus her' situation. I'm sure she feels like I'm very controlling of her phone use, etc. I have controls on the family app of her iPhone, but I do worry about other things she can access. . . ."
>
> **Me:** "She might need to hear you say these honest words. You can admit your fears, apologize for expecting the

worst, and affirm that she's an awesome child and you
want to be a safe place for her to land. Then establish a
joint set of expectations (aka family media plan) so she
doesn't feel ambushed. In this way, parents still have
the option to check usage, but you don't need to exert
that control when other indicators of risk are absent."

The key to a good family media plan is continual conversation. Once your plan is in motion, you might notice that a few rules don't quite work the way you expected, and that's okay (in fact, it's normal). Tweak them. Talk them through with your spouse and kids (in that order). Adjust as you go. The goal isn't perfection; it's progress and consistency! When you've landed on what works, hold that line. Kids are experts at testing boundaries when it comes to screens. So, stay steady, stay direct, and stick with your plan. If you hold that boundary today, you might actually be protecting someone tomorrow—especially the ones who can't protect themselves.

Protecting the Most Vulnerable

When you're building your family media plan, remember this: Always think about the most vulnerable person in your home.

Parents often ask me, "What about my older kids who've moved back in as young adults? What tech rules should apply to them?" My first question back is, "Are there younger siblings in the house?" or "Are there any vulnerable individuals in the home?" Maybe there is someone with a cognitive difference, like my own son who has Down syndrome.

Here's why that question matters: Every digital device in your home, including phones, tablets, laptops, and smart TVs, should be set up to do *no harm* to the most impressionable person under your roof. That's the baseline.

Over the years, I've heard from so many devastated parents who handed a child their unfiltered iPhone to keep them occupied, only to discover later that their child had accidentally stumbled into pornography. The device wasn't filtered or, in the case of an iPhone, Guided Access wasn't enabled to keep a child safe (more on this in the Habit 5 chapter).

In our house, I've learned to assume that any device could end up in my son's hands. That means every piece of tech must be set up in a way that does him no harm because his endless curiosity and quick clicking could enable something harmful to slip through in only seconds.

This is the kind of nuance every family media plan needs. When everyone understands the risks, everyone becomes part of the protection. But that care doesn't stop with our kids; we also care for ourselves by tending to our own hearts. Healthy digital homes often start with healed, grounded parents.

Habit 1 Bonus: Model Healthy Healing

To become an empowered digital parent capable of protecting without panic, we must confront demons that sometimes prevent us from consistently responding with calm and confidence. One of those demons might be sexual abuse you suffered as a child. According to the National Center for Victims of Crimes, 1 in 5 girls and 1 in 20 boys is a victim of child sexual abuse.[15] The intense experience of parenting in light of the persistent dangers of the digital age may evoke painful childhood memories and highlight lingering scars. For instance, reading tragic headlines of digital harm may trigger recall of "unmet needs of comfort, safety, and attunement" in your own childhood. This devastating reality may impact how we parent.[16]

If this is part of your story, I am so sorry. This is a burden no one should have to carry. If you are carrying it, please know you are not alone. This isn't my area of expertise, so I asked a friend, Cindy Robinson, to share what she's learned through her own healing on our Protect Young Eyes blog. Here are excerpts:

You must first heal the trauma that exists within you. Originally, I assumed I was too broken to heal. So my best bet was raising a completely unbroken child and that would be my source for happiness. WRONG. What I discovered instead was, that whatever I wasn't willing to heal I was passing on to my child to have to heal for me. . . .

Tell your child why you tend to overprotect them. Tell them about your abuse/trauma—in an age-appropriate way.

Cindy gives a few book recommendations to help children understand trauma and abuse, then continues:

When it comes to a section of the book that refers to a trauma YOU experienced, tell your child. "That happened to Mama, you know." This is SO powerful. If your child ever does experience abuse, particularly sexual abuse (the most silent and private of them all), who do you think they will tell? The parent who seems perfect, pure, and flawless or the parent who they know can relate? . . .

If you don't heal your traumas, they seep through you in every overprotective action you take. Your child grows up with a scared, distrusting parent . . . Heal yourself—seek professional help, spiritual help, get curious about yourself, whatever you have to do—give yourself the gift of healing. YOU are worth it . . . and your child will reap the benefits.[17]

Please take care of yourself! No switch, app, or filter can replace *you*. The strongest safeguard for your child's digital world is a parent who is aware, present, and willing to step in with both courage and compassion. Protection doesn't begin with a password or a firewall (although we will get to those); it begins with us—our watchfulness, our example, and our love.

But here's the harder question: How can we lead our children into wonder, kindness, and resilience if we ourselves are fractured inside? How can we model calm in the noise of a digital storm if, deep inside, we're still weighed down by baggage that we never asked to carry? So many of us struggle with wounds, sins, or burdens that don't belong to us.

We don't need to find complete healing before we're qualified to lead our kids. That prerequisite would disqualify most of us. But let's *try* wellness. Let's not feel guilty about working on ourselves too. Facing these questions requires bravery, and healing can be a long and imperfect process. Let me encourage you: *I think you can.* If we want our kids to look up with awe, reach out with gentleness, and discover wonder in a chaotic world, a stronger version of us (even if not 100 percent "fixed") might be more successful at showing them the way. Digital calm doesn't just happen on the outside; it starts within us. When we restore our hearts, heal our minds, and have at least a willingness to live free, our kids will notice.

My dear late friend Collin Kartchner often reminded us with a simple but piercing truth: "Showing your kids you love them is 2 percent effort and 98 percent putting down your phone."[18]

Habit 1 isn't about grand, sweeping changes that feel overwhelming. It's about the quiet, intentional micro-moves—those small daily choices that slowly stack into a foundation strong enough to carry a relationship for life. Each moment that we choose presence over distraction and connection over convenience, we are laying the bricks of that foundation.

When that groundwork is in place, something powerful happens. We're ready to move beyond just being present. We can now step into the deeper pursuit of our kids' hearts—and that is where we're heading next.

5 Takeaways for Parents

1. **Let your kids see you live presently:** Model what it looks like to slow down, be fully present, and enjoy real-life moments without constant digital distraction.
2. **Repeat the words that matter:** In a noisy digital world, words that are repeated tend to be words that are remembered (Deuteronomy 6:5–9).
3. **Build your family's tech boundaries on shared values:** Take time to define your family's core values and let those values guide how, when, and where technology is used in your home.
4. **Make small, consistent changes that add up:** Use simple, everyday habits—like announcing your tech use, putting devices down during meals, or asking permission to post about your kids—to show healthy boundaries.
5. **Heal your past so you don't parent from fear:** If you carry past trauma, seek healing so you can respond to your child with confidence and calm, not anxiety or control, and have honest, age-appropriate conversations about your experiences.

"Do Just Two Things This Week" Checklist

☐ Pick two ideas from our discussion about the "sweetness of doing nothing," and implement them this week. Journal about any difference you feel from the changes.

☐ Ask your child to answer three of the seven questions from the family media plan list. You answer the rest and share your responses with your child.

Habit 2: Pursue Authentic Connection

We can grow up in homes in which the food finds the table, the money finds the college funds, and the family even finds the church each Sunday; but somehow our hearts remain undiscovered by the two people we most need to know us—our parents.

—Dr. Curt Thompson

"Dad, have you ever seen a bowling ball crushed?"

Add that to the list of questions I had never been asked until I was approached by my youngest son. He was sitting nearby in the living room watching YouTube videos on the family Chromebook (attached to our filtered router, which you'll learn about in the Habit 5 chapter), and he had just found a channel full of videos showing things being destroyed by an industrial hydraulic press or a massive shredder.

The sight was mesmerizing. Don't judge me until you watch a box of crayons converted into a kaleidoscope of oozing color under a press or watch a 1970s rust-bucket car go through a shredder. I couldn't look away, except to turn toward my son with my eyes wide open and say, "That was awesome," and to hear him respond in a low voice, "I know." We bonded that night over a lot of mashed and mangled goods.

How can tech be part of a healthy connection? In a time when distractions are everywhere, how can parents create a family culture where they are authentically connected to their children? How can they construct a space where their children feel safe and comfortable sharing both the good and the bad—especially uncomfortable digital events? I have a two-word answer: *digital trust.*

Years ago, I was preparing for a parent presentation while sitting in a cafe at a grocery store in Chicago. At that time, I first scribbled down the phrase "digital trust." Seeing how phones, games, and social media were becoming so significant in the lives of young people, I wanted to help parents find ways to build trust in these "places." This then became a key part of our talks. **In homes where digital trust is high, digital friction is often low.**

But how is this culture built? Are there easy steps? Heck, I need to watch a YouTube video to build almost anything, so it'd better be easy. Turns out it's simple—but difficult. It won't cost you anything, but if it's not done well, it is incredibly expensive. So, I've broken down how to build digital trust into five simple yet not simple steps:

1. Don't freak out.
2. Practice curiosity.
3. Tell them what you're afraid of.
4. Side by side: Do tech together!
5. (Actually) practice, practice, practice!

Let's start with the first and most important step, which is sometimes hardest not to do when your kid approaches you with a digital issue.

1. Don't Freak Out

The best way to build digital trust: **don't freak out, don't freak out, don't freak out**. It's a powerful way to maintain trust and to encourage your kids to come to you with anything, anytime. If your child screws up, whether in the physical world or the digital world, ask yourself: Will your disappointment change their behavior, or will it drive them further away?

Moms, dads, and caregivers—your reproach will not change your child's heart. Your anger never produces the outcome it promises. In fact, it almost always leaves a destructive wake. Instead, during mistakes and trauma, our kids need to instantly know the answers to two questions:

- *Am I going to be okay?*
- *Are you still okay with me?*

We often answer those questions before we say one word. The answer first shows on our faces. Then when we do speak, it also shows in our tone.

One mom wrote to me with a tricky situation: Her son had seen what she described as "a picture in a magazine which I don't think was actual porn but rather a very scantily clad woman." She shared, "It was enough that my ten-year-old son confessed it to me months after seeing it. I did the best I could in my response, but I just feel so inadequate. It feels like this first response from me will really set the tone for future incidents where he views something inappropriate." I think a lot of us have been in that position, especially in not knowing what to say, sensing that this interaction could set a path for the rest of the kid's childhood. That's certainly pressure! So, I responded by encouraging her to remain positive, curious, and supportive. She did not need to dismiss the incident, but neither should she dwell on it. I told her: "No need to bring it up again after it happened. Sounds like his sensitivity is tuned appropriately, which is to be celebrated! Just remind him to come to you sooner next time. Well done!"

There's an old quote along the lines of, "You can't see your reflection in a pot of boiling water. Similarly, you can't see truth in a moment of anger." But why bring up anger in an internet safety book? Because the world feels angry right now, partly fueled by our devices. One study found that the tweets from news agencies comprised about 15 percent more negativity than positivity, and negative tweets engaged more users.[1] Anger begets anger.

Let me ask you honestly: Could you be described as angry? Often? If so, your family notices—and your children notice. Do your children feel safe around you? Are they assured that no matter what happens in life, they can land safely with you? Do you want to be a calm, compassionate nest for them to settle into? Do you want to be a strong, steady rock for them to lean on, or a volatile powder keg prone to explode without warning? The anger issue tends to resonate differently between moms and dads. For a long time in our culture, the only emotion many men felt like they were allowed to express was *anger*. We have to purposefully counteract this legacy in our families.

So, let me talk to dads for a moment. From this dad's heart to all of yours, imagine a few things with me.

- Imagine a household where the father is a great stream of encouragement for all his children.
- Imagine a household where the father walks in the door or out of his home office and cares more about what his family needs than how he feels.
- Imagine a household where the father looks for peace, prays for humility, and asks for forgiveness.
- Imagine a household where a father chooses his words carefully. Did you know that most children are radically changed by just a few sentences?

Of course, all these things also apply to moms—not to mention those who are acting as both parents in one, an incredible feat of strength. But, dads, here is a special word for you. Did you know that your words have the unique power to build up or crush your child? They may hold more weight than mom's.[2] Steward your power carefully.

Anger has no place in the heart of a man

- toward his coworkers
- toward his boss
- toward other drivers
- toward his children
- toward his wife

Dad, be calm.

And, moms, I know anger can also live right around the corner for you.

One mom wrote to me:

There was one moment when my daughter was around seven that I had an anger outburst at something one of the kids did. When I was done yelling, clear as day I heard a voice saying, *"Do you feel better? That was for you, not them. Look at them."* The look on my kids' faces broke me, and I decided I would never yell at them to make myself feel better. I had to learn a better way. . . .

I heard a sermon about God that said we have the wrong view of him. We think, "I've messed up; my dad is going to kill me!" But the better view is, "I've messed up; I've gotta tell my dad." Since then, I've tried to tell the kids that this is how I want it to be: That they can come to me with anything and know that I will meet them with love and a soft place to land. The world is harsh and cold, and there's no reason for me to be that way also.

So, wherever you are coming from, don't freak out. Be a soft place, no matter what is going on. Watch your kids reflect calm back, giving you an opening to help them. Your calm is contagious.

2. Practice Curiosity

We've already established that staying calm, or "not freaking out," is the foundation of digital trust. But close behind it is another essential practice: curiosity. Pay attention to your child's digital taps, clicks, and downloads. Yes, even when their choices seem puzzling, trivial, or mind-numbing to you. I may never fully understand the fascination with watching other children unwrap toys on YouTube Kids, but that isn't the point. If they seem to enjoy it, then it also deserves your attention! Entering your kids' digital world with genuine curiosity not only keeps them safer, but it deepens the trust that will carry you both through the more complicated choices ahead.[3]

With tweens and teens, remember that they're surrounded by adults with an agenda all day, especially if they attend school. Dr. Lisa Damour reminds us that what older children really want from adults is our *agenda-less presence*.[4] They would just like us to spend time with them, letting them get into what they're into.

Don't barrage your kids with a ton of annoying questions. While you watch or listen to what they like, they might eventually afford you an opportunity to be conversational and curious. You could ask, *Do all the episodes end like that?* or *What's the toughest boss in the game you're playing?* Your goal is to avoid including consequences, negativity, yelling, or screen time battles in all conversations about technology.

Admittedly, online algorithms may already know more about your child than you do. What your kids google, click on, watch, and replay are all windows into their hearts, their questions, and even their insecurities. (Bark is an amazing tool for knowing more about your child, which you can read more about in appendix 3, "Recommended Tech Resources.") As parents, we can either ignore those digital clues or lean in with curiosity. Choose curiosity! In the end, condemnation does not open doors with your child. Rather, a posture of interest, empathy, and presence cultivates good relationships. That's how you stay one step ahead of the algorithms and create authentic connection.

Just this week, my son opened his school email account on my computer to check for a message. I was standing nearby, and I noticed a message in his inbox from Character.AI, a company named in multiple lawsuits because of its harmful design of AI companions.[5] I could feel anger and surprise welling up in me, along with a brewing "dad voice" just like the one in the father's brain from *Inside Out*. Thankfully, I restrained myself, took a breath, and asked a *curious* question about the AI companion my son had created.

"What have you noticed about this bot? Is it fun to interact with?" I felt bothered that my son was allowed to access this company's website on his school-issued Chromebook, where he had created the account. I was annoyed that our home Wi-Fi didn't block the Character.AI website. But neither of these things was his fault, and we hadn't spoken about the dangers of AI companions (that was my fault).[6] His friends were talking about AI companions at school, and I had not talked about them with him, so he was curious. I would have been too.

Both doors—the door of anger and the door of curiosity—were available to me. The door of curiosity ended up not only being better for my son's heart, but also led to him willingly offering to delete the account without me asking. Small steps—open, curious conversations—and a little bit of progress—these were a powerful combination. Is curiosity a missing ingredient in your tech conversations? It's one of the digital superpowers inside of you! Additionally, did you know that your fears can also draw your children in?

3. Tell Them What You're Afraid Of

For parents of older kids, I have a powerful piece of advice that taps into our fears and leverages them for good. But first, a bit of brain science. When you perceive a threat, your brain triggers its fight-or-flight response and you get ready to react to danger.[7] This is meant to be a temporary state to address an emergency at hand. But today's steady stream of horrible tech news makes it easy for us to become constantly worried parents, and that's not good for our health. So, this is where I ask you, *What are your biggest digital fears?* Maybe you got a start on this question after reading chapter 1. Now it's time to identify and nail your fears down in preparation for opening yourself up to your kids.

Why should you do this? Because your digital fears can either lead you to *spy* or to *speak*. Hold these fears in, and you might be tempted to spy into your kids' digital world. Let them out, and you might open a door of digital trust. Admit everything.

- Are you afraid that they might send a nude photo and totally change the direction of their life? Tell them this.
- Are you afraid that someone with bad intentions is going to send them a DM and lure them into talking? Tell them this.
- Are you concerned about AI companions and their addictive nature? Tell them this.
- Are you afraid they might believe the lies from porn and hurt their brains, hearts, and future relationships? Tell them this.

Please, put these fears out into the light—it's better there! When we do this, such fears automatically have less control over our kids *and*, more importantly, less control over us. This allows us to flip the script on fear and turn it into digital trust. No spying—just speaking. The best way to find digital calm is by articulating the situations that *rob us of calm*. It helps to just say something about it.

One mother named Leah, whose son goes to school with my son, wrote to me sharing her worries about getting her son the iPhone he was campaigning for:

Leah: "My fifteen-year-old can easily get addicted to screens without supervision and has been caught sneaking on them from time to time when he has been told no screens. I know he is getting older and we need to start letting go of the reins a little. But I really just don't know how to do it in a safe and healthy way. And I am so scared to let go. All of your talks I have been to are about safeguards and being smart with technology . . . stuff I have already implemented. Do you have any presentations on how to start letting go of control?"

Me: "Hello, Leah! It's great to hear from you. In your message, you mentioned the sneaking. I believe this is a no-strike move. If you're going to move forward with an iPhone, then there's a zero-tolerance policy for deceptive behavior. He shouldn't be sneaky with a tool this powerful—after all, it belongs to you. So, be clear up front with him about what's expected and what the consequences are for non-compliance.

"And don't forget to tell him you're scared :). It's not because he's bad or not trustworthy; it's because you're dropping him off at a playground with 100 million people. That is a big move for a loving, awesome mom.'"

We can also benefit from verbalizing our fears by realizing that the situation may not be as bad as we thought. As I told one mom, "Maybe you have a good kid!" So, let's prepare our good kids for the worst parts of technology by doing something uncomfortable. Are you ready? (Insert squirming!)

How to Face Your Worst Fear? Make Porn the Norm

Some of you may be shocked by this heading. But stick with me, because it's not some twisted statement about destroying childhood innocence. Rather, it's a statement about making you the authority on something that will otherwise steal their innocence without you. Mom and Dad, when you catch your child looking at porn, remember that they are the victim and you are their safe place.

Ask yourself: Do your children know beyond any doubt that they can land safely and softly with you?

Do they know that there's never a bad time to talk? That they're never in trouble?[8] Do they know this? (Even your sixteen-year-old?)

Think of all the children in your life—your children, grandchildren, nieces, and nephews—do each of them know the answer to this question? If you're not sure, **then I'm giving you forty-eight hours to be sure**. Please, please let them know. Just starting that conversation will give you a better chance of automatically responding with grace and empathy if anything happens. Doing a little homework to understand emotional issues that may come up, such as pornography, is also helpful for you. Let's dig into that specific issue, since it's such a common fear for parents in the digital age.

It used to require planning and focus for a kid to see just one naked woman. The time it took *trying* to see something explicit often far exceeded the actual time you got to see anything. But that's not even close to what our kids experience today.

One study estimated that 27 percent of online video traffic is pornographic, although it is difficult to measure such information.[9] To use an analog illustration, imagine that there were four magazines on the coffee table in your living room every morning when you were growing up. One of them was pornographic, and three of them weren't. And your parents just hoped you didn't pick up the porn magazine. That's what it's like when we give our kids access to anything digital and unfiltered today. Because, as one song goes, "the internet is for porn."[10]

To illustrate this point further, in 2024 alone there were a total of 1,659,051 videos uploaded to Pornhub.[11] The site boasted over 13.5 million videos by the year 2020, including thousands of videos of illegally filmed minors.[12] A recent article reminds us, "Modern porn is unlike anything else in history."[13] Yes, girls also watch porn. And some, like singer Billie Eilish, have bravely stepped forward to talk about the toxic impact it had on their views of sex and their self-esteem.[14]

This is the digital landscape our children are growing up in. But we can't be afraid about this. We can't bury our heads in the sand and just hope our little angel never looks at porn. But whenever I suggest that parents have early, frequent conversations with their children about pornography, I receive pushback because it risks wrecking these kids' innocence and exposing them to information they're not ready for. This is where I need to submit to your authority as a parent because you know the heart of your child so much better than I ever could. Through the lens of that knowledge, do what's appropriate. Admittedly, it's rare to find a parent who talks to their kids about porn *too often*.

If your family is incredibly insulated—perhaps even home-schooling on a homestead—and only infrequently ever hangs out with friends, cousins, or classmates, you might get away with a slimmed-down version of what I'm about to share.

For the rest of us (most of us) who aren't in that situation, I'd like to suggest that we deflate some of porn's power over our children by making it more "normal" by talking about it early and more than once. In this way, you're not making porn acceptable but rather robbing the Enemy of his curiosity power over our kids by making you the authority. Silence on this issue doesn't equate to innocence—and it *isn't* how we create authority.

My family was visiting the waterpark at the Great Wolf Lodge in Traverse City, Michigan, and I was with my three boys in the changing room. One of my boys—I'm not going to say which one—was standing buck naked in front of the mirror and he had his hands over his boy parts. Out of the corner of my eye, I saw him move his hands back and forth in front of his parts as he said: "Porn. Not porn. Porn. Not porn." He moved them away and then covered himself up again. He was eight years old! I just looked at him and said, "Dude, that's funny." I didn't dwell on it—I just smiled and moved on. That's because I've been talking to him about pornography since he was around age five. This is an example of making porn the norm. We want crisp, age-appropriate conversations to happen early, because they are going to need to know what's porn and what's not. If they don't know what it is, eventually they are going to want to find out. And what do they do, then? According to endless messages from parents, they turn to a screen.

One mom—I'll call her Julie—contacted me because her eleven-year-old son had been looking at porn. She didn't know what to do.

Just the week before, Julie was having a conversation in the kitchen with her then eighteen-year-old son about how he was doing. The topic of pornography came up, and they were discussing how it had impacted him. He had struggled with it, but he now had some digital protections in place to help and things were getting better.

But Julie didn't know that her eleven-year-old son—whom I'll call Jason—had been listening to the conversation from the hallway. He heard the word *pornography*, which he didn't understand because they hadn't talked about it. Jason did what any curious young person might do—he went to the family computer and googled the word *pornography*. This happened on a Friday night. Unfortunately, this search coincided with a small window when there were no filters set up on the computer.[15]

Fast-forward to Sunday. Jason was using the computer in the home's small office when his teenage sister walked in on him and caught a glimpse of the screen before he minimized it. His sister immediately told Mom, who was crushed by the prospect of her sweet little boy looking at porn. Dad had left for a business trip and wasn't going to be home until Tuesday night.

Julie told Jason that they would talk about it on Monday. (Imagine how anxious Jason was all day at school!) When they finally talked that evening, Jason said something that Julie didn't quite understand.

"Mom, I just couldn't stop clicking. It was like I wasn't in control anymore."

When Julie heard this news, she felt like the floor had dropped out from under her. A thousand questions raced through her mind, most of them sharp and self-accusing. *How could he just keep clicking? Didn't he know it was wrong? This is a Christian home! He knows better.* Suddenly, the confidence she once had in her parenting began to unravel, thread by thread.

But here's the hard truth: There's more going on beneath the surface of this story. We might quickly ask, "Why was a computer left unprotected, with no filter in place?" But, more importantly, why hadn't an eleven-year-old boy been prepared—especially when an older brother had already faced this struggle? At the end of the day, he reacted as any curious eleven-year-old would have.

I'm not sharing this story to shame a particular parent. Rather, I'm pointing out that families can diminish the probability of harm if we build a culture where frank conversations are the norm. That's why our role as parents matters so much. Early, honest, plainspoken, and consistent conversations about what pornography is—and how to respond when it shows up—arm our kids with the clarity and confidence they need. When we equip them well, they don't face temptation blindly but step into it ready.

If our kids are unprepared, they're at risk. Porn can:

- harm a child's view of sex[16]
- harm a child's view of others[17]
- harm a child's quality of life (risky behaviors)[18]
- cause children to harm other children (peer-on-peer abuse)[19]

For all these reasons, tech-ready families normalize conversations about porn. We even go as far as saying *ten before ten.* Strive for ten "porn talks" before age ten.[20] If you're at a loss about how to do this, or if your fears are keeping you silent, that's understandable. But there's help. Refer to appendix 1, "How to Talk About Porn with Your Kid," for age-appropriate guidelines for kids from five years of age to older teens. It's less scary than you think if you keep lines of conversation open, continue being that safe place, and take a bit of interest in what interests your kids—even if you don't understand it. That's where some tech-ready magic is waiting for you!

4. Side by Side: Do Tech Together!

Raise your hand, if like me, you went through a "work from home" phase where your home office was a recliner in the corner of your bedroom with two TV trays as your desk. Anyone? I'm now blessed with a front room converted into an office with ample space, but it was important for me to have two items in my office other than what was needed for my "work": (1) a couch for my kids to hang out on and (2) a station where all tech is plugged in before bedtime.

I want my kids to know from a young age that technology is so much better as a "we" activity and not a "me" activity.

So, we do tech together. This is sometimes also referred to as "co-play." We've stopped using that phrase because it implies the only way to do tech together is to also be playing something as an adult. But the concept is broader than that. Yes, it's physically shoulder to shoulder, watching videos together and playing digital games together, but it's also just hanging out on Dad's couch while playing the Switch. You are all doing tech together in the same general space.

A mom named Katrina wrote to me, "Your advice has been a huge help with our twelve-year-old. He loves to show us Roblox and never fights when we say, 'Hey, time to shut it down,' and asks us questions about gaming and if we want to see what he's playing."[21]

There's something powerful about having another human involved in your digital behavior. I know this very well because of my past "secret" struggles against compulsive use of pornography. Using accountability software with other caring friends was the secret sauce in my recovery.

I want my boys to see the principle of digital transparency in action from a young age. Scripture begs us to "do" things toward and with *other people*. This is the essence of biblical accountability:

- to be at peace with one another (Mark 9:50)
- to wash one another's feet, or serve one another (John 13:14)
- to love one another (John 13:34)
- to live in harmony with one another (Romans 12:16)
- to have equal concern for one another (1 Corinthians 12:25)
- to bear each other's burdens (Galatians 6:2)

As pastor and author Andy Stanley says, "The primary activity of the [early] church was one-anothering one another."[22]

Jesus Christ modeled "one-anothering" in his earthly ministry, not because he needed accountability but because his doing life with twelve brothers shows us how to live openly and in community. In this way, he shows us the importance of accountability: We are inherently stronger when we are locked together.[23]

However, I was slow in realizing that one of the strengths of the Christian walk is the need to be seen fully by others, online and offline, and to embrace the significance of a God who also sees me. I don't want my kids to have to wait so long to figure this out. So, why not start the togetherness now, in small ways, every day? Don't underestimate the power of your gaze.

Square Up and Look at Them

From the very beginning of life, a baby's brain grows through everyday moments with their caregivers. One of the most important parts of this growth is something called *joint attention*.[24] That's when a baby and their caregiver focus on the same thing at the same time—like when they're both looking at and playing with the same toy. These shared moments may seem simple, but they're powerful building blocks for how babies start to understand the social world around them.

This is true: Babies can tell where our attention is going. One day, I was walking into a Target store behind a mom carrying her infant son, and he couldn't stop staring at me. He wasn't just staring; he was longing for my return gaze. And when I looked back at him and smiled, he exploded with the most amazing big grin, as if to say, "LOOK AT ME! Aren't I the cutest?"

In a recent podcast, author Brené Brown said, "Attention is such an undervalued expression of love."[25] But as children get older, this becomes less natural. Looking someone in the eye becomes a skill that must be taught. And, strangely, amid digital distraction, parents sometimes must relearn this skill.

Looking at your kids still matters.

Whenever I share this statement with parents in our talks, I tell them, "You might think you look at your kids all the time. But parents often tell me how surprised they are to realize how infrequently they square up and look at their kids until they think about it."

We live in a time when our attention is sucked away by our devices. When your kids approach you—the moment you hear their voices—ensure they know *they* are more precious than the device they're competing with. Prioritize this, even if you must verbally clarify that you just need to finish typing an email so you can give them your full attention. As Dr. John Delony says, "Your child is more important than your phone. Never, ever give them a reason to think otherwise."[26] So, look right at your kids.

Oh, and frequently give your kids a bonus. Put your hands on their shoulders or, even better, gently hold their face and say, "I sure do love you. I'm so proud of you and love being your dad (or mom)."

For older kids, Dr. John Delony says, "Hug them and hold your hand on the back of their head. These simple actions can down regulate your kid's nervous system, help their body relax, and help you be deeply present with them."[27] You are together, side by side, eye to eye, hand on head. Make doing tech together part of doing life together, because actions do a lot of the talking in a tech-ready family.

5. (Actually) Practice, Practice, Practice!

According to Swiss child development expert Jean Piaget, children ages 0 to 11 are still developing the ability to use abstract logic and reasoning.[28] During this stage, children understand time and space but not as independent concepts, so we must attach our instruction to concrete situations. This means, act it out! Such an approach is especially true during ages 7 to 11, when we're often having more conversations about appropriate use of technology, but even our teens are going to gain clarity from practicing what we want them to do. So, act things out often! This is especially important in digital situations that deal with pornography, sextortion, and predators.

First, let's cover the situation that often creates the most concern in parents—pornography. It's not enough to just tell young kids, "If you see porn, here's what you do." We must also *physically* show them what we want them to do.

In appendix 1 of this book, you'll find the rule "Put it down and tell someone." It's a simple rule to give any kid for when they experience something online that makes them feel funny, off, or wrong. So, how do you practice it? You could sit your child at the counter or on the couch with a device such as a laptop or tablet, or in front of the smart TV. Then say,

> I'm going to the bedroom and closing the door. From there, I'm going to yell, "Go!" and I want you to pretend you see something scary, violent, or inappropriate, or someone doing something weird—anything you know isn't right and good. Then I want you to put down the screen (if it's a laptop) or turn off the screen (if it's an iPad) or turn off the TV (if it's a smart TV), walk up the

stairs, knock on the door, and say, "Mom, Dad, I saw something wrong. I want to talk about it." Remember, it's *not* your fault, so let's practice.

This is, again, so simple but so, so effective.

This same principle of "practice" works with digital secrets—something we don't want kids to keep. There are only two okay secrets—parties and presents. We probably need to tell someone about every other secret. *So, honey, if someone does something or tells you something other than parties and presents, and tells you to keep it a secret, what will you do?* (Tell someone!)

Like with shooting free throws, practice, practice, practice is important. For your tween, who might be home alone more often, practice may look like, "I'm going to pretend I just came home from the store. If something happens on a device that hurts you, is wrong, or is inappropriate, I want you to tell me when I walk in the door." Then you go outside, wait ten seconds, walk in the door, have them practice the words, and practice your response.

But this isn't just for young kids. Moms and dads, square up and look at your teen sons. Get their full attention.

Son, this iPhone is amazing and awful—all in the same package. It's connected to all the people that love you as well as millions who couldn't care less about your life. I need to make triple sure you know what to do if something goes south—no matter how horrible it is. First, no dick pics. [Yes, I'm being intentionally provocative here—get his attention.] Ever. Never put anything into this phone that you wouldn't send to the admissions office at a college. But if you find yourself in a bind, no matter what, promise you'll wake me up and tell me. I need you to say it. Say, "Mom, Dad, I'll wake you up, no matter what." [Then practice.] This is going to feel juvenile, but I also want you to say, "Mom, Dad, something really bad just happened. Can you help me?" Please say it right now. I need you to say the words and hear yourself saying them, so that you can press this memory into the thinking part of your brain when the feeling part of your brain is telling you to run and hide.

(The practice isn't just for them. It's for *us* too.)

According to researcher Michael Slepian, "One of the biggest reasons we keep a secret is that we feel shame around it and fear we'd be judged if it came to light. The more immoral we feel our secrets are, the less likely we'll share them with others."[29] This sense of shame can be amplified further if we listen to the Enemy's voice in that moment, which can intensify our desire to keep the secret. That's exactly what sin often does—it ruptures relationships with those around us who love us the most and turns us inward instead of outward. The devil loves keeping kids quiet.

Be sober-minded; be watchful. Your adversary the devil prowls around like a roaring lion, seeking someone to devour. (1 Peter 5:8)

This is why it's so critical to work with our kids in frequent, tangible ways and give them tools that point them toward help. If we don't practice, young children will believe the lie *I'm going to get in trouble. I need to keep it a secret.* A tween or teen might believe the lie *I'm such a screw-up.* We aim to destroy those nagging whispers and strengthen our tech-ready family with repetition and physical practice. In doing so, we also decrease the risk that our nice kids feel bad about walking away from a dangerous digital chat. After all, online predators are often some of the "nicest" people.

Talk About Tricky People

Most of us knew not to talk to strangers when we were kids. I was five when Etan Patz was abducted in 1979, signaling a kind of "end of innocence" for children. Parents like mine then started telling us to avoid people we didn't know who had puppies and candy in white Chevy vans with few windows.

In other words, we identified strangers based on what they looked like. The little hairs on the back of my neck would surely stand up in the presence of a person with bad intent. At least, this was the theory.

Fast-forward to today. Kids are physically safer than ever because they rarely leave the house! But today's digital parks are infinite in number, and kids spend time in them from the comfort of their bedrooms. Therefore, we now teach our kids to identify strangers not by what they look like but rather by what they talk like. Since everyone looks normal and friendly online, looks are no longer sufficient. Instead, we tell our kids about tricky people.

Here are some tricky people red flags, suitable for discussion with your elementary or middle school child:

- Tricky people are people whom I don't know who are very nice to me. Some of the most dangerous people on the internet are also some of the nicest people on the internet. They might say, "You're very pretty. Has anyone ever told you that before?"
- Tricky people are people whom I don't know who ask me questions. They want to know things about me so that I will trust them. They might say, "What things do you like? Do your parents ever make you mad?"

- Tricky people could invite me to use a different, more secret platform. They might say, "What's your Snap name? Can we talk more over there?"
- Tricky people might seem a little pushy when I try to stop talking to them. They might say, "Hey, why won't you respond? Don't be mean to me like this."
- Tricky people ask me to keep things a secret: "Just keep this between us." But tell your kids that there's no such thing as a good digital secret.
- Tricky people might offer me gifts for no reason. They might say, "Do you like Robux? I want to send you some money as an early Christmas present."
- Tricky people might threaten me so that I'll do something I don't want to do. They might say, "Send me nudes or I'll tell your parents something bad about you."
- Tricky people are intently looking for kids who express any type of emotional distress. When they see kids posting about having a bad day, hating their parents, or experiencing a breakup, that's when they sweep in with empathy and understanding. They might say, "Oh, my parents are the worst too. What happened?"

After you've gone through this list, give your kids permission to walk away from anyone, anytime, for any reason. Tell them that they're in control of the conversation. Remind them that if they don't know the person *off* the internet, they don't talk to them *on* the internet.

Ask yourself: Does my *really* nice kid know how to walk away from a *really* nice predator? If not, give your kid permission to walk away (and practice it). If you don't do this, walking away can feel mean for kids, and many of them don't like to be mean.

Maybe say this exact statement to your six-to-thirteen-year-old child: "Walking away from an uncomfortable conversation online isn't mean; it's smart."

Just like with "the porn talk" shown in the previous section of this chapter and in even more detail in appendix 1, you're teaching your son or daughter to "put it down and tell someone." This approach allows these two awesome statements to be easily applied to multiple digital situations. That's what we've discovered—simple and consistent practices often add up to big protections for our kids. In a world where digital answers are quick and unfiltered, let's regularly turn our kids back to ourselves as the authority. You care about your kid's heart more than Google.

Ask: "Do You Need to Google Me?"

Every summer for over five years, my son has gone to Boy Scout summer camp. It's a week spent in a remote camping center in West Michigan, full of activities with around four hundred other tween and teen kids. What could possibly go wrong?

For the summers when I don't attend with him, I drop him off, give him a hug, and habitually say, "Hey, have a blast. And I guarantee that while hanging out with the guys, there's a good chance you'll hear something we've never talked about. That's okay. But when I pick you up next weekend, I'll ask you the same question I asked last year: 'Do you need to google me?' [as in, ask Dad, not Google]. Be curious with me; I care about you more than YouTube, Google, or ChatGPT."

After all, kids talk about a lot of things. Because of technology, they have access to a massive amount of mature information daily, which is so easily shared with other kids on the playground, on the bus, or at summer camp. A few times a year, there will be a mature show on Netflix—examples over the years have included a drama about young people and suicide or an international "deadly challenge for money" show—and kids talk about it. It is good to remind our kids to bring their curiosity to us and often follow up with them about this. You could do this activity during car time, mealtime, or bedtime. These are perfect windows for us to work on our "practice, practice, practice" routines.

Finally: Remember, They're Still Your Amazing Kids

As we work through the five steps toward building digital trust that you just read about, we must often be reminded to listen to the right voice. Pursuing authentic connection means that we stay mad at the tech and not at our kids. Here's a social media exchange I had with a mom that resonated with many of our follower parents when we shared it.

> **Mom:** "I just caught my eleven-year-old looking at Pornhub at 2 a.m. I'm totally heartbroken and don't know how to recover from this. I have been crying for an hour trying to figure out what I did wrong. Where did I fail him? I thought he was my innocent boy—but he's apparently not. I feel so betrayed and don't know what to do when daytime comes. . . . My heart breaks when I think about how many times this has happened. I don't think I can sleep at all thinking about this. He was very scared that I caught him. I can only thank God for keeping me up until 2 a.m. and that I saw him through my living room camera. Heartbreak doesn't even begin to explain what I feel."
>
> **Me:** "Hello, I'm so sorry this happened . . . Where are things now?"
>
> **Mom:** "I talked to him after I calmed myself down. He said the material popped up before while searching for something—he doesn't fully remember what he was looking for. I thought some details were off. He said he thought of looking at the images at that time. This made me wonder if it had happened before—but he said no. I can't keep pushing even if I feel he's not telling me the truth. I reassured him that I'm not mad at him; I'm mad at these websites that tempt kids and

steal their youth. We came up with a plan that devices including laptops will be in my room every night. He is not allowed to use the computer for a month, and even when he does it must be in a specific place. He can still play his Nintendo or PlayStation 4—but no computer.

"I can't fully trust him at this time, and I still cry when I think about it. This is a mom's worst nightmare and biggest heartache. I feel I look at him differently now because he's not as innocent. I wanted to ask you—at times I wonder if this episode means more to me than to him? After I had my talk with him, he seemed happier and relieved, like a big weight was off his shoulders, and he wasn't too scared anymore as compared to when I first caught him. And he apologized right away during our talk. I guess I'm wondering if maybe for him seeing the material was just a fleeting thing of curiosity and now he's over it? But as for me, I can't get past it. I feel like I am to blame, and I do blame myself for it. But it would probably take a long time for me to recover from this—and he seems back to normal."

Me: "Thank you for sharing. What you're experiencing sounds like what often happens when a husband admits a porn problem to his wife. He feels so much better because it's off his chest and in the light. But her world has been shattered, and her trauma is just beginning. I suspect that if your son feels better that maybe it was happening for a little while. But I'm so glad he's acting 'lighter' and freer—you can celebrate that! Now it's time to lock down doorways. There shouldn't be any way for Pornhub to enter your home on your network . . . It's a process of making sure everything that depends on Wi-Fi gets connected to the

Gryphon router [More on this in the Habit 5 chapter] . . .
**But above all, please, please remember this. He is
STILL your amazing son."**

Mom: "Gosh, you're gonna make me cry again."

Me: "It's ok. This is tough."

Mom: "Yes, as I mentioned, it's hard to look at him without
thinking of what happened."

Me: "You don't need to stuff things away, so it might be
important to find your own counseling here, but
he must not sense that you think there's anything
different about him."

Mom: "Thanks for letting me know that I am not the only
one feeling defeated, guilty, and needing a reminder
that he is still my amazing son. It's hard to trust. It's
like when he says one thing, I always doubt it. I don't
want to bring up what he did or use it in a judging
way . . . but I still find myself crying whenever I think
of it. I just need to keep clinging to God's truth and
promises."

Digital trust is such a multilayered issue. It can feel simple, but
it's also not simple. Remember: Grace first! Let your kids know they're
still loved and cherished. And also get the counseling you need to deal
with your feelings related to issues like this. Have the same mindset
as the father in the parable of the prodigal son (Luke 15:11–32). He was
just glad his boy was finally home. If our children sense that same
gladness from us, we will create the authentic connection that's so
powerful and critical in the face of an onslaught of insane technology.
When we gain connection through the tactics shared here, it's like
the flu shot that decreases the risk of contracting the virus. It softens
the impact because our kids can come to us quickly before shame
and secrets become toxic. This is how you get your relationship *and*
your home tech-ready and help your kids find *their* digital calm in the

middle of their digital storm. And as we consider Habit 3, you'll be surprised at the power that non-tech activities have in preparing our kids for a very techy world.

5 Takeaways for Parents

1. **Stay calm, stay connected:** Authentic connection is built when parents remain calm, show empathy, and avoid yelling—especially during difficult digital situations. Calm responses build digital trust.
2. **Build digital trust:** Trust grows through three key actions: (1) Don't freak out; (2) be curious without judgment; and (3) share your digital fears with your kids instead of spying.
3. **Talk early and often about porn:** Conversations about pornography should start early, be age-appropriate, and happen frequently so parents—not the internet—are the authority.
4. **Practice and prepare:** Regularly rehearse responses to digital dangers with your kids. Practice "put it down and tell someone," and use real-life scenarios to build confidence and safety.
5. **Pursue, don't pull back:** Despite adolescence being a time of natural distancing, strong parent-child relationships are vital. Show up, lean in, and reassure your kids that they're loved—no matter what.

"Do Just Two Things This Week" Checklist

☐ Remind your kids—even the older ones—that they can land safely and softly with you. Then say it so often that they roll their eyes and finish your sentences!

☐ Physically "practice, practice, practice" a safety routine related to technology with all your children.

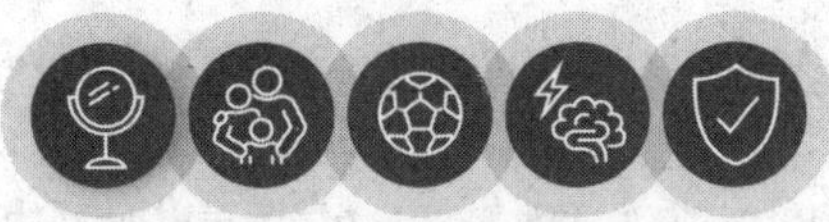

Habit 3: Encourage Work and Play

Play is often talked about as if it was a relief from serious learning. But for children, play is serious learning. Play is really the work of childhood.

—Fred Rogers

Neurophysiologist Rodolfo Llinás wrote about a brain-eating marine creature in his 2002 book *I of the Vortex: From Neurons to Self*.[1] No, this isn't some monster prowling the ocean searching for sailors to devour. Rather, he told the story of the sea squirt, which is born with a simple eye, a tail for swimming, a spinal cord, and a primitive three-hundred-neuron "brain." Shortly after being "born," the sea squirt quickly finds something solid to attach to, like a rock, and never moves again. Once it settles, it consumes the parts that are no longer necessary for survival: its tail, simple eye, spine, and brain. *Who needs a brain if you're no longer moving?*[2] It might as well rot.

Have you heard the term *brain rot*? It was named Oxford Word of the Year in 2024! Lovely, right? Between 2023 and 2024, searches for the phrase "brain rot" increased 230 percent, which caused Oxford to add the term to its full online dictionary. Brain rot is defined as "the supposed deterioration of a person's mental or intellectual state, especially viewed as the result of overconsumption of material (now particularly online content) considered to be trivial or unchallenging."[3] You can almost picture our kids' little brains withering away like raisins in front of their screens. Preventing our children from contracting "brain rot" and experiencing the sad fate of the sea squirt is the basis of Habit 3: *We encourage work and play.* Why is this a part of making a tech-ready family? It's about building a life outside those devices that's more attractive, rewarding, and *real* than anything the digital world could offer. Remember: Young brains are built, not born![4] The job of childhood is to wire up the brain[5]—and this happens best through movement.[6]

Ready to Work

I first met Melissa Griffin, the "HR Mom," in early 2020 when we teamed up to create the "Pandemic Parenting" virtual conference during the opening days of the COVID-19 lockdown. I loved her relatable, commonsense approach that was born out of real-world, corporate experience.

On her website, Melissa describes something stunning that she noticed while working on hiring teams for Fortune 100 companies:

> Over the years, I watched the skills and capabilities of young workers decline, while their managers became increasingly baffled by the realities of the entry-level workforce. Again and again, we hired smart, academically-successful young adults, who looked great on paper. Once on the job, many experienced crippling anxiety and lacked the confidence to make decisions on their own. The more I examined these trends, the more clear it became that many popular modern parenting styles were hindering our kids' ability to successfully navigate the real world.
>
> I realized that if more parents would put in the work to build these skills while their kids were still at home, this talented new

generation would have the confidence and capability to step into adulthood.[7]

How does Melissa build up her own kids' skills? "I always start with chores," she says.

On the surface, giving your kids chores is an easy way to decrease your workload as a parent. But it's deeper—you're also setting them up for future success.

As part of Harvard's ongoing multigenerational Grant Study that started in 1938, researchers analyzed the backgrounds of more than seven hundred "high achievers" and found a clear link between doing household chores as children and achieving success later in life.[8] This makes intuitive sense. When kids take part in shared responsibilities, *they feel more connected to the family unit*—a kind of ecosystem—which boosts their self-esteem. This also teaches them to recognize the needs of others and be more inclined to offer help.

Although screen time wasn't conceived when the Harvard study began, there's a strong connection because kids often go to screens to find a sense of belonging, to be "seen," and to feel needed. Consequently, chores can remind them that they are needed and that they belong in the home, where they're an important part of the team. The household doesn't run quite the same without them.

In other words, kids grow up less self-centered when they contribute to their household. If everything is done for a child, they may assume the world revolves around them. In contrast, contributing builds humility and a sense of duty. It also fosters a strong work ethic—which I know from experience isn't always natural but can absolutely be taught. (My parents instilled it in me, even if I didn't appreciate it at the time.)

These lessons translate into greater career success: increasing teamwork, empathy, discipline, and the ability not just to lead but also to follow. This experience helps us raise kids who have a better shot at becoming less dependent on screens and more productive adults.

Slowing the Dopamine Loop

When kids sink hours into TikTok, Fortnite, or YouTube Shorts, their brains are riding what neuroscientists call the *dopamine loop*. Dopamine is a neurotransmitter—the brain's reward chemical—that spikes when we encounter something novel, exciting, or pleasurable. Short-form digital content is engineered to hit that loop over and over again: bursts of color, sound, and surprise. Each spike injects a quick "feel good" rush but is followed by a crash, leaving the brain restless and craving the next hit. This cycle can wire kids for impatience, distraction, and compulsive scrolling.[9] Other fast-dopamine examples include:

- **Social media:** Liking, commenting, and scrolling through new content
- **Eating sugary foods:** Consuming sweets and processed foods
- **Video games:** Winning a game or achieving a high score
- **Online shopping:** The thrill of making a purchase
- **Gambling:** The excitement of placing a bet and potentially winning[10]

Slow-dopamine experiences lead to a more sustained release of dopamine, "contributing to long-term satisfaction and wellbeing."[11] Examples include:

- **Exercise:** Regular physical activity, such as running or yoga
- **Reading:** Immersing yourself in a good book
- **Learning new skills:** Picking up a new hobby or learning a new language
- **Completing challenging projects:** Finishing a work project or a DIY task, like my son adding a whammy bar to his electric guitar
- **Meditation and mindfulness:** Being quiet and present
- **Human connection:** Engaging in meaningful conversations and activities with loved ones[12]

Think about the activities that truly shape us—building a tree-house board by board, practicing an instrument day after day, or training for a 5K one mile at a time. These are the slow, steady steps of executive functioning[13]—the mental muscles that help us plan, persevere, and finally reach a goal. When we encourage our kids to embrace work like this, we're not just keeping them busy; we're training them for life. That perseverance will show up in their marriages, in the grit it takes to finish a massive project at work, and even in the patience required to landscape a backyard. The truth is, very few meaningful things in life deliver instant rewards, and almost nothing worthwhile operates on TikTok time.

Part of Habit 3, encouraging work and play, is teaching our kids the beauty of *delayed gratification*. As a runner and as an athlete, I always had to buy into this idea. Some days began with me not feeling like getting up and running. But by noontime on a day when I did get my bottom out of bed and start pounding the pavement, I was thinking, *I am so glad I pushed through and did that*. At first I didn't want to do it, but I ultimately got satisfaction from a job well done.

To teach our kids about this type of perseverance, *we* are often the ones who need to get out of the way. As parents, we sometimes act out of a pure but misguided motivation to not make our kids unhappy or to work too hard, so we do too much for them. Sure, we feel good about the clean room or the perfectly folded laundry we can present to our precious kids—but we've robbed them of an opportunity for *them* to feel that satisfaction, haven't we?

Let's face it—we can do the work better than a kid. And faster. And to our liking. But here's the thing: It's okay if the mowing lines are crooked and the plates and cups aren't stacked perfectly in the dishwasher. When my son filled the dishwasher for the first time, stacking dishes on top of each other, I could clearly see that stuff was going to fly around once the water got going. That ramen noodle dish was going for a ride! But he was so proud of his first attempt. I had to let it be *his* first attempt without correcting it and making it more *my* attempt. Although it was a bit of a mess, *if I re-did what he did, I risked UN-doing his confidence.*

So, we have to be okay with an imperfect execution so that our amazing kids can experience the deep pride that comes from effort, not perfection. It's the kind of pride no video game can give. Stumbling and bumbling through childhood wires their brains for resilience.[14] Dirt under their nails, sunshine on their faces, scraped knees and all—these are the experiences that help our kids grow sturdy in both body and spirit.

Ready to Play

Just like work, play is an essential part of human existence. In fact, play is part of a kid's work. For the first few years of life, play is essentially their full-time job. And if they don't get it? Serious things can go wrong.

Dr. Stewart Brown is the founder and past president of the National Institute for Play. In 1966, after one of the nation's first mass shootings, Brown was part of a commission investigating what led University of Texas student Charles Whitman to murder seventeen people. He discovered that Whitman experienced play deprivation, or an "almost complete suppression of normal play behavior," according to the commission. Brown went on to study inmates guilty of violent crimes and found that almost none could provide abundant examples of free play in childhood.

Brown came to a provoking conclusion: The lack of rough-and-tumble play in childhood had shaped these inmates' well-being and development. "The adaptive tolerance and empathy toward others that is learned in early preschool through rough and tumble play is really a fundamental part of our having tolerance for people who are different than we are," Brown said.[15] So, play isn't just something nice to have—it's essential. Let's make sure our kids get what they need.

Free-Range Kids

My elementary school years were spent in a typical neighborhood in Lansing, Michigan. As the oldest child, I was the experimental focus for my amazing parents, who were juggling three other kids by the time I went to kindergarten. Many of the kids who attended Post Oak Elementary lived in my neighborhood and walked or biked to school every day. I wasn't alone—my friends Bryan and Eric joined me for the half-mile walk—and a steady stream of children traveled the entire way, all heading to school. All by ourselves.

Things have changed a little since then, haven't they? This is clear in the story of Lenore Skenazy, who in 2008 was living in New York City with her husband and nine-year-old son, Izzy. Like many New Yorkers, they didn't have a car and rode the subway as a family all the time. This meant that Izzy knew the subway, their usual stops, and generally how to navigate the process. So, he started asking his parents if they would take him somewhere in the city they hadn't visited before and let him take the subway home to flex a bit of independence. Skenazy explained, "I think [this] is the suburban equivalent of, like, 'will you take me to the library and let me ride my bike home?'"[16] They decided to let him try it.

Skenazy and her husband put some thought into the starting point by taking Izzy to Bloomingdale's, which has its own subway stop downstairs, decreasing some of the complexity compared to leaving him at Grand Central Station. Izzy just had to go downstairs and get on the subway, which is exactly what he did, emerging a few stops later at Macy's on 34th Street, where he took a bus across town to their apartment. According to Skenazy, he was "levitating with pride and a sort of excitement and that feeling you get when you've done something and you can't wait to say, 'I did it!'"[17] Izzy felt very special in front of his parents as he shared an incredible landmark achievement in his annals of childhood.

And that was it. At the time, Skenazy was a writer for the *New*

York Sun, but she didn't even think to write about this episode until a couple of months later when she had no other topic to explore. Her new article was literally read around the world. It was entitled "Why I Let My 9-Year-Old Ride the Subway Alone"—and sparked a global firestorm of reaction from both sides. Many people could relate and reminisced about their childhood freedom, but others quickly awarded Skenazy the epithet "America's Worst Mom."[18] Anxiety-ridden, "worst-first thinking," helicopter, lawnmower, and stealth fighter parents were united in their criticisms.

But the threats of child endangerment Skenazy received only "intensified her desire to encourage anxious parents to give their children the freedom they need to develop the self-confidence and resilience to cope effectively with life's many challenges."[19] This led to the publication of her book *Free Range Kids: How to Raise Safe, Self-Reliant Children (Without Going Nuts with Worry)*, a blog with the same name, and a thirteen-part series on Discovery Life Channel called "America's Worst Mom," where she intervenes to rescue families wrought with anxiety, including a mom who still spoon-fed her son at age ten. "Worst first thinking has become so habitual that it feels like it's instinct," Skenazy often remarks.[20]

But what if our children are smarter and stronger than we think they are? What might happen if we let them go a little more free-range in their play? It's a risk, sure. But how will they "wire up" their brain if we never let them move their bodies?

Play Contributes to Childhood Happiness

I have vivid memories of recess at St. Thomas Aquinas School, where I spent grades one through six. I also remember a steady stream of injuries that resulted from recess time, like when my friend Art fell from the monkey bars and broke his arm. He got a cast, and we all signed it. In fact, there was almost always some kid in class with a cast on *something*. A recent social media post from a Gen X comedian reflected on how his elementary school classroom often felt like a VA Hospital infirmary full of bumps, bruises, casts, and injuries.[21]

Not anymore. Do a search for a "good choices/bad choices" poster for the playground, and you'll see items that include 75 percent of what I remember at recess:

- no playing in the mud
- no standing on swings
- no climbing up slides
- limit your yelling

What in the world is playtime, if not these things? And what kind of impact is this attitude having on our kids? In 2023, Drs. Peter Gray, David Lancy, and David Bjorklund published "Decline in Independent Activity as a Cause of Decline in Children's Mental Wellbeing: Summary of the Evidence" in the *Journal of Pediatrics*. Feels like the title says it all, no? They begin the article with "two very well-established and disturbing facts:"

- Children's freedom to play and explore has declined greatly over the last half-century.
- Children's mental health has declined greatly over the last half-century.[22]

I talked about potential reasons for why parents are increasingly careful in chapter 1. Unfortunately, in combination with digital pressures, we are going down a road we don't want to travel. Part of being tech-ready is not just removing toxic tech to protect our kids' mental health; it's adding in play and exploration, an antidote to so much toxic tech. We're helping them develop life skills, relational intelligence, and physical coordination, which are not found in an endless scroll of YouTube videos but instead in the fresh air of nature.

Play Outside

"It's better to kick a rock down the road than to scroll," according to a counselor friend of mine. Accordingly, I find that movement through creation is soothing to the soul. It can shake a few new nagging things loose in our minds.

As I reflect on my own life, I can spot activities that have brought me peace and calm during life's storms. Have any of these helped you?

- prayer
- sleep
- nature
- exercise
- strong friendships
- strong family support
- mindfulness
- breathing

Even if you don't accept that social media and tech overuse *causes* mental health declines, there's almost universal acceptance that the list I just posted *helps offset* stress and anxiety.[23]

Take exercise, for instance. In one study that observed the effects of exercise on anxious students, researchers concluded that hard exercise teaches your body that an elevated heartrate means something other than anxiety, reassuring the brain that feelings of intensity aren't always noxious.[24]

Exercise—or exercise disguised as play, like running races, playing a pickup game, or just letting kids run around like little maniacs—elevates endorphins, sometimes referred to as the runner's high.[25] But aside from endorphins, exercise regulates all the neurotransmitters targeted by antidepressants, including norepinephrine. Exercise wakes up the brain and improves self-esteem, which is one component of depression. Exercise has also been shown to boost mood-improving dopamine and feelings of wellness, and it jump-starts the attention system.[26] Even prisons value the benefits of fresh air; the United Nations Standard Minimum Rules for the Treatment of Prisoners states:

> Every prisoner who is not employed in outdoor work shall have at least one hour of suitable exercise in the open air daily if the weather permits.[27]

How many of our kids get less time outside than some prisoners? Time outside and moving around can be the best kind of play. This is not just an antidote to a tech-saturated world; it prepares kids' minds and brains to face the world by being stronger, happier, and better balanced. But things become more complicated when other families aren't on the same page. So, how do we start judgment- and conflict-free conversations with other parents about screen time, devices, and what "healthy tech use" really means?

Playing with Friends: Conversations with Other Parents

I hope you're convinced by now of the value of work and play. And if you're thinking about giving your children more unstructured, real-life, outside play, that's great! It's the work of childhood, after all. Unfortunately, we no longer live in a world where it's possible to recreate the idyllic, analog romping about the neighborhood you might remember without some thought about digital risks. We have to think of whom our kids will be around.

What about kids who carry unprotected phones? What about families that have different tech rules than ours? These are good, valid questions that demand relevant responses.

I grew up in a conservative, religious home. If I was going to spend time at another house, I remember my mom wondering if that family had Showtime, Cinemax, or HBO, because I wasn't supposed to watch those channels. She had to know this detail before I could go there.

Fast-forward to a recent talk I gave to a mom's group at a local church. Talks to such groups are some of my favorite presentations because these moms of younger kids are often the ones fully responsible for daily digital protection. At the end of the presentation, one mom shared that her elementary-aged son had started hanging out with a group of kids and at least a few of them had their own smartphones. In general, today we often know far less about the families connected to the kids that our kids spend time with. This is very different from what I remember in my younger days; my mom was BFFs with the parents of most of the kids I romped around with. I shared these words in response to this woman's concern: "Hey—maybe parents need to get back to having the courage to gently approach other parents, calmly but directly, and discuss tech expectations."

Her response left me speechless. "You don't understand—I'm a millennial. We don't do that; it's too uncomfortable and I don't want to come across as judgmental."

This retort is a real thing. Since then, I've encountered it many times. But I have to ask: Are we really considering the risk of inaction compared to the risk of having an awkward but necessary conversation?

I'm sure my response was equally shocking to her: "This might feel uncomfortable to hear, but if an adult is going to choose to have children and be a parent today, then this is just part of our responsibility. This is the gig! It's what it takes to protect our children from potentially life-changing digital trauma."

In my experience, other parents are often relieved when you start the conversation about technology as your kid and theirs are spending time together. Some are afraid of being the "bad cop," and so you give them permission to make *you* the bad cop.

So, go for it, bad cop! You can have this conversation, *even if* it feels uncomfortable and judgy. What does such a conversation look like? It's slightly different from the "Showtime, Cinemax, HBO" question I remember growing up—but it's even more critical to have it today.

Here are a few questions I like to cover with parents when my kids are spending time at their house.

- **"What are your digital device rules? I want to ensure that my son obeys what's important to you."** This is a great first question, because you're immediately showing them that you're not motivated by judgment but rather by a desire to honor what's important to them. Parents have told me that this sometimes gives them information they can build on in follow-up questions.
- **"Do you think the kids can have some time offline first, and then they can go online later? We're trying to find a bit of balance at our house . . . I feel like I'm the never-ending bad guy."** This one comes from the Screen Sanity website, which catchily calls it "the playdate preamble."[28] This is another good example of leading with a question to soften the judgment.
- **"Here's what my son has with him and what's on it."** This is another example of warming up the conversation by just stating what, if any, devices your son has and the filters or controls that are on it. This can sometimes open curiosity in the other parents if you describe what your kids are using and they've never heard of it.
- **"Are there any unfiltered devices in the home, like iPads?"** Now we're getting into more technical, bold territory—but iPads are just big iPhones. If they say yes, gently share your rules for those devices.
- (If you're feeling good and confident) **"Is your Wi-Fi filtered?"** This question most often spurs curiosity in another parent because so few even know that routers can be controlled (more on this in the Habit 5 chapter). But maybe you'll have an opportunity to share more if they seem open. This question is critical if your child starts to spend a lot of time at the home, including sleepovers.

My kids simply can't spend time with other kids unless I know answers to these questions. Why? Because it only takes one website to traumatize a child and I'm not willing to take that risk. Some parents have told me they are so nervous about their child spending time at another house that they've decided to make their home the "hangout zone." They've taken very intentional steps to have activities, games, and a space where their kids and their friends can have a good, screen-free time. They have a device basket at the door and have let parents of the kids who come over know the process. If some parents push back because they want to get in touch with their kid, maybe just a talk/text device is allowed to be kept (Gabb, Bark, Troomi, etc.). That is simply the rule.

Remember that your child is only as safe as their friend with the "weakest" digital rules. Accordingly, being on the same page with their friends' parents can help decrease the risk of harm. But since digital doorways are everywhere, conversations with parents are just the start. What tools might your kids have in case something slips through?

Playing with Friends: Conversations with Our Kids

Of course, you won't always be able to talk to the parents before your child interacts with other kids. So, it's important to equip your child with tools in his or her digital belt so they're ready to hang out with other kids as safely as possible.

Here are a few things to teach kids, starting at around elementary-school age.

- **"What do you want to show me?"** When another kid approaches your kids with a device and wants them to look at something, prepare them to ask this question before taking a look. Tell your child that if the situation feels weird, then it probably is. Don't look first! If the other kid tries to get pushy and show them the screen anyway, they can interrupt the "transaction" with the statement below.

- **"We don't look at other people's screens."** This is a stricter variation of the first question that can decrease risk even further. It is also a good statement to "practice, practice, practice."
- **"If it feels weird, then it probably is."** Your kids can repeat this statement to themselves, and you might also put it in your cycle of phrases to say often. Remind them that their feelings matter—they may even be a bit of a superpower—and they can listen to that little funny feeling in their stomach. That's Holy Spirit radar that might be beeping to let them know, "Hey! Be alert!" When that radar starts to go off, the next statement follows.
- **"Put it down. Tell someone."** Remember "practice, practice, practice" from chapter 3? This statement is a key one to rehearse often, and part of that process is agreeing on a list of "someones" whom your kids can tell if anything online or offline makes them uncomfortable.

For slightly older kids, this process can be trickier. I once had an exchange on social media with a mom whose daughter's friend was watching Pornhub. Fortunately, the daughter said something to her mom, but this left the mom in a tough spot.

Here's our conversation:

Mom: "Hello Chris, I need some advice please . . . I am a parent to a thirteen-year-old girl. I have had many open conversations with her about smartphones, social media, sex, porn, etc. She does not have a smartphone. (She has a Pinwheel.)

"Her best friend does not have any type of phone but told my daughter this week that she uses the computer (or iPad) at home. She watches sexual movies like *Fifty Shades of Grey* and also came across Pornhub. She was telling my daughter about it and that she should watch it . . . My daughter said her friend would get in so much trouble if her parents knew. What do you recommend I do as a parent? Do I tell her mom? I would want someone to tell me if the situation was reversed. But then I risk affecting the girls' friendship and this girl being mad at my daughter for telling and breaking trust. She is smart and erases the history on the computer."

Through a series of back-and-forth DMs, I recommended that this mom's daughter gently share information about human trafficking and Pornhub's horrific track record of child sexual abuse. She patiently waited for the right opportunity. A week later, I received this follow-up message:

Mom: "I thought I would update you on what happened with my daughter and her friend. My daughter spoke with her friend, and she received it very, very well! She had no idea that what she was watching was even called pornography or that it was bad. My daughter told her friend that she had told me (although she was very worried her friend would be mad at her), but to her surprise she was not mad at all and was thankful. A few days later, I was able to speak to both girls about this and her friend was so thankful and open with me. She shared that she does not know about any of this stuff since her mom does not talk to her or tell her anything, so she looks it up—poor girl. I explained that the way the internet is going to show us things is not accurate and will harm us. I highly encouraged her to talk to her mom. I am not sure if she has yet—and I may still talk to her mom as well—but it turned out so wonderful, and I am SO SO proud of my daughter!!!!"

It was so worth it to this mom and her daughter to press through the discomfort and awkwardness and start that conversation. Wouldn't you want to know if something like this was happening? As this next mom discovered, not being told was crushing:

Lindsey: "My son's innocence was abruptly ripped away from him at eleven when an older child in the neighborhood showed him and other children aged eight to twelve, including his little sister, pornography. This went on for weeks, and my son eventually confided in a friend, who told his parents, who contacted me. Imagine if he hadn't told—how long would this have gone on? None of the other children told. Our next-door neighbor also found that this older boy had put Pornhub on her son's iPad. She never told us; she didn't want her son to be the tattletale. She could have stopped it at that point! These were trusted neighbors, and confronting this family was the hardest thing I've ever had to do. The knowledge that I let my son down will haunt me forever. All my precautions and restrictions and homeschooling and like-minded friends—gone in an instant."

This is so crucial—don't be that parent who doesn't say anything! Press through the discomfort and worries of sounding judgmental. Open that conversation with grace and humility, but be intentional. Be that safe space for kids. You can prevent harm to both your own kids and others' and protect that sacred space of playtime with friends that's so critical to children's development. We can also apply these tactics to other childhood experiences—birthday parties are *supposed* to be fun, not risky!

Playing with Friends: Handling Birthday Parties

Party time is the ultimate playtime, right? That is, unless the phones are also invited. Try charting a different path by learning from my experience and mistakes.

One weekend, we had six friends over for my son's thirteenth birthday and we didn't know many of the parents because most of these friends were new. So, here's what we did. It wasn't perfect, but a good amount of it worked well.

- **First, outline your expectations.** To remove any surprise for my son, I told him beforehand that when his friends arrived, I was going to ask each parent if their child had a phone. These phones could only be used to communicate with parents while the party was ongoing.
- **Second, put everything in writing.** On whatever is handed out or sent to parents, state your expectations clearly on the invitation. I did miss a key detail—asking parents to talk about these expectations with their kids before dropping them off. Also share your phone numbers on the invite. (They needed these details anyway to call/text us in reply to our invitation.)
- **Third, be the welcome wagon.** When kids are dropped off, stand in the driveway and greet each parent. Introduce yourself and ask, "Does your child have a phone with them? Great— while they are here, I'm having the phone kept away." Then I asked the parents, "You have our phone numbers if you need anything, right?" Thanks to the invitation, they did.
- **Fourth, announce and reannounce.** With all the kids hearing the same thing, we made our expectations known initially

in the house and then a second time in the van on our way to the party location at the corn maze.

If I had to do this again, I would have collected the phones in a basket in the van during the thirty-minute drive to the corn maze, just to make that separation clearer for the kids. I wrote about this experience on Instagram and asked our followers: "Have you had kids over for a party? What has worked for you?" One offered this good question:

> I like this idea as the host, but if my kid were the guest I'd feel torn with not being able to get in touch with them privately, or possibly uncensored, especially if I didn't know the other family or attendees. I would want my child to be able to contact me immediately, without asking for permission, should need arise. Have you had parents push back or not be comfortable with this arrangement?

Some other readers replied with great solutions, such as allowing a child to have a smartwatch or locking down a phone so they could keep the device on themselves. The main thing would be having a calm, transparent conversation with the host to come to an agreement. Again, focus on that open conversation and work out helpful solutions so our kids can have good, safe fun.

It is possible for your kids to play with other kids without feeling powerless against this wave of unregulated tech. With some intention and courage, you can make play safer for both your children and the kids they're enjoying life with.

The goal isn't to eliminate all screens but to ensure that a child's non-screen life is rich with other forms of engagement and connection. Being a tech-ready family means helping your child approach work and play intentionally, building muscles of resilience and patience. When your kids play with others, they learn boundaries and courage. When they work through a list of chores, we give them the benefits of delayed gratification and being part of a family that works and plays together, pushing through resistance to get to the good stuff. Habit 3 builds up the strength of their hearts and minds. A well-rounded childhood with ample opportunities for physical and social activity is one of the best ways to prevent future screen problems and support healthy development. It equips children with the foundation they'll need to combat the pull of addictive technologies. We will explore ways to resist this attraction in the next chapter.

5 Takeaways for Parents

1. **Overconsumption of digital media dulls development:** Like how the sea squirt digests its own brain once sedentary, excessive screen use ("brain rot") is mentally numbing, especially for youth. Encouraging work and play helps combat this stagnation.

2. **Chores and responsibilities build essential life skills:** Teaching kids to do household chores fosters time management, empathy, a strong work ethic, and resilience—traits critical for career and adult success. It also helps reduce their dependence on digital entertainment for self-worth.

3. **Unstructured play is crucial for mental health:** Decreased opportunities for independent, child-led play correlate with declines in children's mental well-being. Activities like outdoor free play build creativity, problem-solving skills, social cooperation, and emotional resilience.

4. **Equipping kids to navigate screens safely with friends:** Children should learn simple, practiced habits such as asking what they're being shown, trusting their instincts if

something feels wrong, and "putting it down and telling someone" so they can respond safely when peers show them inappropriate content.

5. **Parenting requires courage and intentional boundaries:** Parents must be proactive in setting tech expectations at home and with other families. Difficult conversations and protective digital habits (e.g., device-free zones, monitored screen access) are necessary to guard against harmful online exposure.

"Do Just Two Things This Week" Checklist

☐ Identify a task you're doing that could be handed off to one of your children.

☐ Practice one question from the "Playing with Friends: Conversations with Our Kids" list.

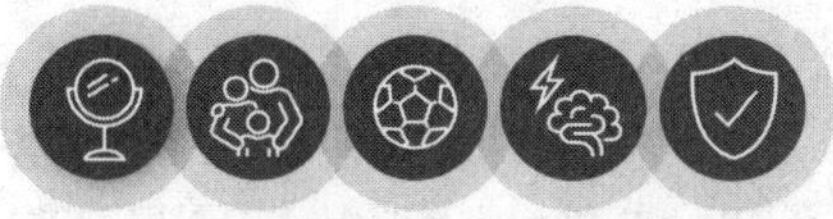

Habit 4: Delay Addictive Technologies

When you can't put it down, that is a perfectly
predictable response to a perfectly tuned machine.

—Sherry Turkle

Do you know anyone who gets hungry?

In 2010, Snickers kicked off its legendary "You're Not You When You're Hungry" marketing campaign on Super Bowl Sunday with a trash-talking Betty White, and it blew up fast—going global and lasting over a decade. A long list of actors including Danny DeVito, Elton John, Robin Williams, Aretha Franklin, Willem Dafoe, and Danny Trejo turned into an alternate version of themselves before they took a bite.[1] We all identify with them, because we know what it's like to see someone become a whole other person when their brains and bodies are in reaction mode. Our amazing brains are responding to internal and external stimuli all day long, triggering reactions ranging from "eat the candy" to "keep scrolling hilarious videos." Kids and adults have this in common. Yet, on other levels, we tend to forget that our kids' burgeoning brains and bodies are operating differently than ours. It takes a lot less stimuli to trigger them into losing control (but that's not their fault).

I've heard parents say a lot of things over the years in response to these conversations about tech, such as:

- "Kids are resilient. Why worry so much about this?"
- "I love video games. I see no problem playing them with my son."
- "I looked at my share of porn growing up and I'm fine."
- "I don't understand why my child turns into a rage monster when I take the iPad away."

On the surface, these comments make sense—they're real and relatable. But if we look closer, each one reveals the same problem: Most of us are missing key pieces about how kids' brains work in today's tech-saturated world.

This gap in understanding matters. It leaves us unprepared to guide, protect, and raise healthy kids in a digital age.

What does the actual research say? What do we know now? It points us toward a clear strategy: Delay kids' access to what I call "addictive technologies." That's why we say, **no smartphones until they get *into* high school** (eighth grade is too soon) and **no social media until at least age sixteen**. Or, to put it another way: **#delayistheway**. But why? Why has this been part of our parent script for *years*? Because it's hard to overstate just how addictive today's technologies are to our kids. As we explore Habit 4, we'll find out how the brains of children are significantly different from the brains of adults and are consequently uniquely vulnerable to this kind of tech. We'll then learn what to do about this.

Is Tech Addiction Really a Thing?

Doctors and researchers disagree on whether problematic *technology use* rises to the level of an addiction, as defined by medical professionals. We most often associate addiction with substances such as alcohol and drugs. The DSM-5 (*Diagnostic and Statistical Manual of Mental Disorders*, Fifth Edition) uses eleven criteria to identify substance use disorders; here are some of them:

- Trying to cut down or stop using the substance but being unable to.
- Experiencing intense cravings or urges to use the substance.
- Developing withdrawal symptoms when not using the substance.
- Neglecting responsibilities at home, work, or school because of substance use.
- Continuing to use even when it causes relationship problems.
- Giving up important or desirable social and recreational activities due to substance use.
- Continuing to use despite the substance causing problems to your physical and mental health.[2]

Just two or more of these criteria are required to diagnose a substance abuse disorder.

Do these behaviors look familiar? Any of us who have seen a child or adult struggling to let go of social media, pornography, or gaming have observed similar signs. According to a summary of the *Handbook of Children and Screens*, "Some health professionals classify [these] as behavioral addictions: **problematic internet use, gaming disorder, and dysregulated smartphone use**. Like traditional addictions, these conditions are recognizable by the way they impair users' life functioning, and the distress users feel during cessation."[3]

What do we mean by "addictive technology"? Pornography, social media, most games,[4] YouTube, and even some "educational technology" *can* be very addictive. If it's free, then it's probably built on an algorithm to keep you engaged with customized content and serves you advertising. We are "the product," and some—particularly young brains—may find those digital spaces uniquely addictive. Remember that PhDs, data scientists, and researchers are building these apps,[5] and they don't have the same goals as us. They also understand the human brain—especially the one inside of your child.

Neuroscience: Three Levels of the Brain

Every conversation about technology *must* include a conversation about the childhood and adolescent brain. So, let's get down to it.

The human brain is the most amazing machine in the universe. Adolescents "are not just smaller adults. They're in a different phase of development, and they're in a critical phase of brain development," said former United States Surgeon General Dr. Vivek Murthy.[6] He's right. The brain has four hundred miles of capillaries[7] and one hundred billion cells.[8] It is endlessly complex yet amazingly simple, having three functional areas that we'll refer to as the reptilian or "lizard" brain, the limbic system, and the neocortex.[9] These three clusters of brain activity work together toward similar objectives. Understanding these functional areas will help us deepen our knowledge of our amazing kids and educate us about why they sometimes click, tap, and scroll in certain ways. So, let's dive in, shall we?

Level 1: The Reptilian Brain

First, the **reptilian brain** (or, vividly, "lizard brain") is the ancient, primitive part of our neurology located deep inside at the base of the brain. It primarily oversees regulatory functions. For instance, if your body temperature goes up, it senses this and causes you to sweat. If you're cold, it makes you shiver. Dr. Robert Sapolsky calls this "everyday, shop keeping stuff."[10] The reptilian brain also interacts with thirst, sexuality, hunger, and hormones. We're certainly thankful that it does these things automatically so we don't have to put "release neurochemicals" on our daily to-do list. It's operating effectively from birth, keeping us alive with the basics: poop, pee, cry, and eat. Your child's brain is asking the important question *"Am I safe?"* on this level.

Level 2: The Limbic System

The next layer out from the reptilian brain is all about feelings and emotions: the **limbic system**, a massively important grouping of brain structures including the amygdala, hippocampus, and basal ganglia. We experience stress, anxiety, arousal, and fear in this system. We also find the reward pathway and the neurotransmitter that gets all the attention in the digital age: *dopamine*. Why is dopamine important? If something outside of us is perceived to be good for us, dopamine gives us focus, motivation, and memory so that we'll interact with that thing over and over again. On the other hand, when danger occurs, the limbic system imprints a memory so that we avoid this hazard in the future. Because these behaviors are connected to our survival, these responses often occur automatically and unconsciously in milliseconds. (You might have heard about the fight-or-flight response, which occurs here.)

The limbic system is also the part of the brain that fuels connections. Have you been in the room when a baby smiles for the first time? The whole room seems to light up! Even mean people stop and smile at babies. I believe it's because we're biologically tuned—created—to give a baby emotional affirmation that he or she is okay. We also want to show this precious little person that interacting with other humans is good, smiles are good, and emotions are good. You almost can't help yourself—it's in your limbic system! This system says *connect*, and we are rewarded with that hit of dopamine.

Although we are emotional beings from birth, the limbic system is on fire during adolescence as the developing brain longs to find a like-minded "tribe" to connect to and feel supported by. Think back to chapter 1 and the statements from Dr. Winston, such as, "The teenage years are when the need for social connection is as powerful an instinct as hunger." Teenagers are seeking to answer a very different question: *"Am I loved?"*

Don't forget this information, because Silicon Valley is full of billion-dollar tech companies that understand the adolescent limbic system. In fact, you'll start to notice that almost everything engaging and exciting about social media is a limbic-system-activating feature.

Level 3: The Neocortex

Finally, there's the **neocortex**, uniquely sophisticated in humans compared to other species. It is responsible for reason and conscious intellectual thinking, but is subservient to the limbic system until well into our twenties. Our children are not there yet. This region of the brain is asking the question, ***"What can I learn?"***

As we discover how the adolescent brain works, let's remember that Level 2, the limbic system, is where our kids are mostly operating. This means they might not always make the most logical decisions. But do you know why?

"What Were You Thinking?"

During adolescence, the brain is all go and no slow. It's like a nitrous-powered street racer with the brakes from my minivan. Risk, curiosity, impulsivity, and action are the name of the game—this is why some teens jump off things that adults only take pictures of. When confronted with a risky situation, we might think, "That's dangerous, you might get hurt!" But that's such an old-person statement—that's the neocortex talking. In contrast, your teen is thinking, "I might be popular! It might feel awesome!" That's the limbic way of thinking because its focus is, "Am I loved?"

So, the next time you observe young people doing something completely irresponsible and ask in an exasperated tone, "What were you thinking?" now you know they aren't! And at that age, you also weren't. Teen brains haven't changed that much. It's easy to see how—like a carrot and a stick—the reward circuitry is easily fired up in apps such as TikTok, Snapchat, or Instagram that have features promising a quick return.

You can also see how a reward incentive can be so easily weaponized by our technology. Let's take the issue of sextortion in the tragic case of Jordan DeMay, which I mentioned in the introduction of this book. Sextortion is one of the most devastating issues enabled by social media features that connect bad actors with vulnerable and sometimes extremely impulsive young people, especially teen boys. Why? It's because their reward-sensitive and socially sensitive brains are easily triggered into sending something inappropriate when a reward is dangled in front of them.

I have been very open with my strong feelings about Snapchat, and here's why: Its core features, like disappearing photos and instant communication, are a perfect predator to the adolescent brain. Their fireworks light up the reward center, pushing that "send it now!" impulse and feeding their fear of missing out. It's dopamine on demand.

When I had the opportunity to speak privately with Snap's CEO, I pleaded with him to do more to protect kids from their own neurological vulnerabilities. I told him, "Because of where teens are in their neurological development, they are uniquely sensitive to limbic system responses. And Snapchat is a turbocharged, neurochemical, limbic system force."

The truth is that our tweens and teens were never meant to go head-to-head with this irresistible tech. It's not a fair fight—and the consequences can be devastating. For example, we're seeing too many young people who have died by poisoning from drugs sold to them on Snapchat.[11] "Quick add" (a Snapchat friend-adding feature), quick choices, quick hits.

Friends, when you understand the adolescent brain, you see teenage behavior differently. For instance, when I see a teen who can't quit playing Fortnite, I say to myself, "That's mostly not their fault." When I see an anxious teen trying to keep the Snap Streak going, I say to myself, "That's mostly not their fault." When I see a teen hopelessly hooked on porn or unable to put TikTok down, I say to myself, "That's mostly not their fault."

According to school resource officer David Gomez, "Giving your kid social media is like bringing home a baby dragon—adorable at first, but it can quickly get out of control and burn down the house."[12]

Now that you understand a little more about how your kids are wired, maybe your empathy and compassion are also growing. Their brains aren't broken! They're amazing, powerful, and still under construction. Their impulsivity isn't a bug; rather, it's an amazing feature. That's why they need us to help them navigate the deceptive, addictive pull of the tech world that was never designed with their protection in mind. We not only can help them prevent harm but also point them toward more meaningful answers to some of life's big questions.

Developing Identity and Meaning

Adolescence is a season of searching. It's a time when young people begin to wrestle with the deepest questions of identity and belonging: "Who am I?" and "Where do I belong?" These are timeless questions asked by every generation—and maybe you've also asked them. But in past decades, the number of voices attempting to provide answers has been relatively small.

Voices like family, church, friends, teachers, and the occasional pop culture influence like MTV or VH1 were far from perfect, but the dominant voices often belonged to people who genuinely cared about you. They knew your name, your story, and your potential.

Today, the landscape is different: Our kids are surrounded by a thousand competing "mirrors," each reflecting a distorted version of who they should be. Some of these kids are understandably confused and anxious. Others are swapping identities and feelings like clothing. Ten thousand digital mirrors with ten thousand thoughts, voices, opinions, and distorted ideas are blaring at them 24/7. We call these *influencers* for a reason.

That's precisely why hearing trustworthy voices matters. During this critical window of development when identity is being shaped and cemented, our children need to hear fewer voices. They must tune in to the voices that care most about them—thoughtful, grounded, trustworthy voices that help them see themselves clearly and affirm that they belong.

Because of social media, there are too many mirrors and too many choices. During a time when our kids need less input, we give them exponentially more. When we need to level up their opportunities for human connection, we level up their digital connectivity. When we need them to look up in wonder, searching for the divine, we compel them to look down, searching for the selfish. When their fabulous but fragile version of "self" is coming online, we groom them to completely break away from offline life.

It's simply too much, too soon. Many kids don't know how to handle it all.

Too Much, Too Soon

Kids don't always have a category or container in which they can put a lot of the things they encounter. I remember what that felt like. On January 28, 1986, I was sitting in Mr. Kopke's room with the rest of my sixth-grade classmates, all watching the space shuttle *Challenger* launch. It was a special mission because a teacher, Christa McAuliffe, had joined the crew. But just over one minute into the launch, the world witnessed the shuttle explode and the booster rockets fly untethered toward the Atlantic. We looked around, unsure if we should believe what we watched. Nothing made any sense.

Even NASA Mission Control fell silent in disbelief.

For years, the space shuttle had launched without any issues. I was particularly fond of space, planets, and the shuttle because my uncle worked at NASA and often sent me pictures of our solar system and rockets. But the shuttle violently breaking up after takeoff didn't have a "category" or place in my brain where I could make sense of it. No one had ever talked to me about that being a possible outcome, which left me anxious and confused.

In today's world, how much more do our kids encounter confusing—even horrifying—things without receiving feedback from anyone about what's going on? **We call this "content ahead of schedule."** Children process new information by categorizing it based on their existing knowledge and developmental stage. When they encounter content that is too advanced for their understanding— whether it's a disintegrating space shuttle, overly sexualized media, intense themes in movies, violence, or complex adult issues—they struggle to find appropriate mental categories to store and process this information. This premature exposure can disrupt their natural development, causing confusion and emotional distress.

My friend and counselor Michael Reiffer explained it to me this way: "I can't give you something that you're going to have to categorize without first giving you categories where you put it. What do I file it under? What category does this go in if I get something so beyond where I'm at? It's like sugar for a newborn to a [young] mind. It's so activating, thrilling, all sorts of stimulating, but there's no category to file it under. It's super difficult to put it away, neurologically."[13]

For instance, if a young child is exposed to pornography around age ten, ahead of puberty and maybe ahead of sexual education, he's now seeing graphic images and thematic content about what grown-ups do but has no way to understand it.

According to Reiffer, kids will say things like, "I don't know, were they wrestling? I thought I was possessed. My heart was beating out of my chest. I felt electrified!" because they don't know what to file it under. They don't understand intimacy and marriage, and they have no category for what they've seen.[14]

Content ahead of schedule isn't just porn; a long list of online and offline content is thematically "too much" for young minds. Here are some other examples:

1. **Intense adult themes:** Movies or stories involving life-threatening situations, substance abuse, or extreme psychological struggles are beyond the comprehension of young children. Exposure to such themes can result in misinterpretations and a heightened sense of fear and insecurity.

2. **Violence:** According to the Youth Endowment Fund, which surveyed 7,500 British children ages 13–17, 60 percent of children witnessed real-world acts of violence on social media in the last year, 25 percent saw content promoting violence against women and girls, 47 percent reported that violence and the fear of violence impacted their day-to-day lives, and 20 percent said they'd skipped school due to feeling unsafe.[15] Of course they're afraid; they can't understand what's happening.

3. **Adult responsibilities:** When children are forced into roles of responsibility too soon, such as managing household issues during a parental divorce, they can develop stress-related symptoms like sleep disturbances, stomachaches, and behavioral changes.[16] They do not have the emotional maturity to handle such situations.

4. **Shocking world events:** For example, Sandy Hook (or any school shooting), September 11, 2001, and the *Challenger* disaster. There's a reason we rush a team of counselors into schools and communities after such events—we know that children need help processing their emotions. They've been exposed to something and they're not sure what to "do with it."[17]

When such stressful situations occur, young brains can experience disruption.[18]

Here's another example from my conversation with Reiffer:

It's like when you have stuff on the kitchen counter. Or on the steps going upstairs. And every time you walk by the counter or the steps, there's that "thing"—the bill, the schedule, the towel—it's sitting there. The mess is there and it bothers you until it's "put away." That's a simple way for a parent to try and understand what's going on inside a young brain. It's disruptive and stressful. But multiply it—what they're feeling is more intense because they have much fewer coping tools.[19]

How does this look in real life? One mom shared an example with me:

> **Amber:** "I am a parent of young kids (infant, pre-K, and K) and I am also a fourth-grade public school teacher. I just left a parent meeting with a student who has significant mental health needs. This student gets on YouTube during the night and watches inappropriate, creepy, and scary videos. This causes her to have terrifying nightmares where she's doing things such as killing people. Then she doesn't sleep and comes to school and rages (refuses to work, yells, begins choking herself, throws things, runs out of the classroom, etc.)."

This poor young girl does not know what to do with the too-soon material she saw, and she cannot cope with it. Yes, you could say that kids are resilient—but we do have a responsibility to guard them against tech that will disrupt their brains and to protect their development and the joy in their childhoods.

We're pressing hard on what's happening inside of amazing young brains because our efforts give us reassurance that #delayistheway is worth the work. Anyone who decides to "delay addictive technologies" is going to experience headwinds from friends, culture, and even family (sometimes family is the toughest opposition). But when you start stacking your growing knowledge of the tech and your kids, you also start building your confidence that your gut has been right all along. "Right tech at the right time" is the right thing.[20]

Putting It Together: How Brains and Tech Intersect

Compared to where you were when you started this chapter, how's your knowledge of the brain? It's a lot to take in, I know. But I hope you're more empowered to make tough tech decisions because you know more about what's going on in your kid's head.

This knowledge also helps us understand how apps are constructed and how intensely they affect our children. Let's take Snapchat, for example, and its infamous Snap Streak:

> When you and your friends Snap back and forth with each other at least once a day, every day, you're on a Streak! Once you've kept it up long enough to start a Streak, you'll see a fire emoji on the Chat screen. . . . If you see an hourglass emoji next to the Chat [for example: 3 🔥⏳], your Streak is about to expire! To keep the Streak going, make sure you and your friends each send each other a photo or video Snap ASAP.[21]

Remember, the core question of the limbic system, especially during the tween and teen years, is "Am I loved?" And now we have a feature that creates a fraudulent correlation between the length of your Streaks and the quality of your relationships. The risk of breaking the Streak causes you to worry (still within the limbic system's sphere), activating your stress response and a release of cortisol, the brain's stress hormone. This prepares the body for action—either "fight" or "flight." If you're a young person with a brain flooded by cortisol, facing the risk of breaking the Streak, the most effective way to bring your body back into balance is to open Snapchat and keep the Streak going. This feels safer to the brain than breaking the Streak.

Snapchat is undoubtedly very aware of the teenage stress response, and the Snap Streak undoubtedly wasn't created to improve the *quality* of friendships. Instead, it established a whole new qualifier for whether you're a good friend—"How long is your Streak?" By knowing how important the Streak is to some kids, the company has monetized anxiety.

Snapchat's website gives more details:

Snapchatters will each receive one free Streak Restore. After that's used, the price shown on your device is the price that you'll be charged if you choose to restore a Streak. The cost to restore a Streak will vary in different countries.[22]

And people will pay that charge!

If you can't quite believe this, listen to my next example. After a talk I gave at a high school in my hometown, a young man approached me to share about his experience with the Snap Streak. Jayden was honest about how much it controlled him. He wasn't looking at porn or struggling with mental well-being. **He just couldn't stop thinking about maintaining his Streaks.** His longest Streak was over three years with some random person, and he obsessed over keeping it going. Like kids in my own youth ministry, Jayden paid friends to keep his Streak going when he didn't have access to his phone. The Streak finally stopped when he had his phone taken away as a punishment and no one could log in for him in time to keep it going.

Officer Gomez told me that one of the most frequent requests he receives from juveniles he locks up is whether they can somehow keep their Streaks going. Take a minute to absorb that!

Jayden allowed me to make a video of him sharing his story. We did some simple math and calculated that he spent maybe around 150 days' total time using Snapchat during the time of the Streak. He lamented what he could have done with 150 more days of life.

Jayden wanted to be seen and connected, so his limbic system just wouldn't let him *stop* thinking about the Streak. In the same way, it's easy to see how TikTok's lure of virality so easily entraps young (and older) brains. It's well-documented that Instagram's feed is a steady stream of perfect, polished, beautiful, put-together images that seem to have a more toxic impact on teen girls than teen boys.[23] The nagging, constant question of "Am I pretty enough?" is a persistent whisper for many young girls. We've already read in chapter 1 about what Meta did for its own financial gain with data about young girls deleting selfies through the sworn testimony of Sarah Wynn-Williams.[24] This means we should not be surprised to find charts showing reports of female self-harm that look like hockey sticks.[25]

Imagine growing up where:

- Tragedy trends. The news about it is constant.
- Popularity is quantified.
- Porn is ubiquitous.
- Your worst moments are magnified.
- Social comparison impacts your self-worth.
- You were given a supercomputer (i.e., an iPhone) without much training.
- You're punished for misusing your supercomputer. *Wait, didn't my parents give it to me?*
- Your parents constantly use their phones.
- Godlike apps study your every move.
- Neuromarketing manipulates your behavior.
- Your brain makes all these digital experiences seem so good in the moment.

Can you see how everything fits together? These aren't just bad or broken kids being naughty with an iPhone. Good and strong kids are having their choices hijacked by supercomputers. These are not normal times, and so our response must be out of the ordinary. Regular habits do have power, and we apply them little by little for most things—step by step and chat by chat. But you also have the power to make big changes when necessary. Why? Because you know what all this tech is doing to your kids, and you know how the brain works. Yes, tech can be used for good! But we must constantly ask ourselves if it's worth the risk of causing harm. That's our motivator behind delaying access to addictive tech. So, let's take some practical steps in Habit 4 to bolster our new understanding of the brain and feel more confident in our tech-ready decisions.

Find Your Like-Minded Tribe: The Birth of #delayistheway

A teacher named Ashley wrote a note of thanks to me for being bold enough to encourage families to delay introducing tech, even though everything in culture is pushing in the other direction. She said, "As a teacher I see the effects of tech every single day, which has caused me as a mom to delay all of it as long as possible. It's overwhelming to try to keep up and stay ahead to keep kids safe." I know many feel the same way. Thankfully, there is help out there that gives, as Ashley put it, "hope that I stand a chance at surviving this as my kids get older." We find more hope by being protectors together.

Since 2015, we at Protect Young Eyes have been telling parents to delay smartphones and social media. Other movements like Wait Until 8th also brilliantly spread this message. Then one afternoon in September 2021, I was inspired to make a social media post using the phrase "delay is the way." It rhymed, and it stuck![26]

#delayistheway is a *slow* tech strategy, not a *no* tech strategy. And even if we've said *no*, our kids still need to *know* how to navigate tech. It's a mindset that reminds us to:

- ignore pressure
- ignore culture
- ignore fear
- listen to your gut
- listen to science
- listen to childhood—their #onepreciouschildhood

Listen: There are certain hills that I'm willing to die on. One of them is that our children cannot be the best versions of themselves emotionally, spiritually, or relationally with the presence of social media in their lives. There is no long-term risk in *not* exposing our children to interactive media.

As many in the child digital safety space say, I've never been approached by a parent who regrets giving their child Snapchat too late. Instead, they fight against the collective action pressing them into allowing social media too soon. And the best way to fight collective-action problems is with an offsetting collective-action solution. We must band together on this.

So, parents, wherever you are, *find your like-minded tribe.* A global movement of parents deciding to wait on tech together is popping up everywhere. For instance, the Wait Until 8th movement started in Texas in 2016 when its founder, Brooke, felt the pressure from tech and asked other parents to join her in waiting until eighth grade to allow smartphones. More recently, we've seen the Smartphone Free Childhood (SFC) movement in the United Kingdom utilize Meta against itself by gathering parents in WhatsApp groups to feel the power of positive community. Country-specific SFC groups in the United States, Ireland, Switzerland, New Zealand, and others are growing. There are also groups in Australia (Wait Mate) and in Mexico (Moviemento No Es Momento and Delay Smartphones MX). In the United States, these groups often start among parents with children in the same class at school. I'd love to see churches also encourage the same collective action among members who are parents. Just think: Could you join or start a group like this in your spaces?

Kids Don't Mind Waiting—Really!

Even though parents can be nervous about how their children will respond or are hesitant to be the bad cop, some kids understand and appreciate the boundaries their parents place.

Being part of a group can help you keep hope alive by hearing stories like this one, from a mom named Stacey:

I have a nine-year-old girl and an eleven-year-old boy, and we have never allowed any sort of video game console in our home. My son wants to have a sleepover for his twelfth birthday, and I told him that we could borrow a PlayStation for the night so he could play *Madden* with his friends. He very quickly responded, "What? No, Mom, I don't wanna ruin my party with video games!"

I think kids appreciate boundaries around video games and social media and smartphones. While it has been challenging to be one of the only families in our area that has these boundaries, my husband and I continue to be more confident than ever in our decisions around these devices.

Here's another story from a second mom, shared anonymously:

My fourteen-year-old (who doesn't have a phone) was telling us rules she would have for her own kids one day, and she listed "no phone until sixteen years old" as one. I said, "Wait, does that mean you actually think it's good we won't let you have one?" And she said, "Yeah, I do. I know I complain sometimes about it, but I really honestly think it's best."

Let's give a high five to these families and to all families who join the movement to delay so that their kids can enjoy their childhoods even more!

What if it's too late to delay? How can we walk a decision back? Appendix 2, "Is It Too Late to Delay? What If My Kids Already Have Tech?" has your mindsets and steps.

Straight Talk About Video Games

Both adults and kids get hooked on video games (ever seen *Candy Crush* gems when you close your eyes?). If you are thinking of freeing your kids from this addictive tech, you're joining the many parents who are dealing with situations like these:

> **Kerry:** "My fifteen-year-old son is asking to play *Fortnite*. We have never allowed this game in the past. A lot of his new friends seem to be playing it and he'd like to connect with them. (We moved into a new town a year and a half ago.) My son is in tenth grade now. What do I do?"

> **Rachel:** "I'm worried about desensitizing and normalizing violence. I used to tell my boys that you can't respawn in real life . . . kinda in a joking manner but actually dead serious. . . . I'll never forget the time I caught my nephew pretending to shoot pedestrians in a nearby park. We were driving and he seemed to be reenacting a drive-by shooting from a movie. We found out he had been playing *Grand Theft Auto 2*."

Game designer Sam Liberty has admitted that even though he had knowledge of "dark patterns" in video games, which are designed to trick you into taking action, his eight-year-old unknowingly subscribed to a "premium" coloring app that cost eleven dollars per week.[27] Game developers are creating "compulsion loops" on purpose.

Parents, we are a long way from our Atari days, when *Pinball* and *Space Invaders* were as intense as it got. Today's video games are much more sophisticated.

In a chapter about "addictive technologies," video games demand a significant yet complicated conversation. Studies have shown us a good amount more about the impact of social media on young people than about the effect of video games on players. Consider the following contradictions:

- **Related to mental health:**

   A study by the National Institutes of Health found that children who played video games for three or more hours daily performed *better* on cognitive tasks involving impulse control and working memory compared to non-gamers.[28]

   But:

   Some studies have shown that excessive gaming can lead to issues such as addiction, social isolation, and increased aggression, negatively impacting teen mental health.[29]

- **Related to social connection:**

   Online video games can help individuals build friendships and social skills, especially for those who may find in-person interactions challenging.[30]

   But:

   While video games can be a coping mechanism, they may also contribute to social isolation if they replace real-world interactions.[31]

- **Related to violence and aggression:**

   Research from the University of Oxford found no correlation between the play of violent video games and increased aggression in teenagers.[32]

   But:

   One analysis concluded that violent video game play is positively associated with aggressive behavior, suggesting a link between game content and aggression.[33]

What should parents believe? Some experts suggest removing video games from children because of their addictive design.[34] Others promote more nuanced approaches to video games, depending on the child.[35] But in spite of these varying opinions, here is our position at Protect Young Eyes: Based on what we know about the brain, child development, variable rewards, and our yearning to connect (that potent limbic system!), today's video games *should not be taken lightly*.

So, if you're going to say yes to today's video games, it's important to understand *what else you are saying yes to*. For example, it's difficult to "stop" a *Fortnite* match once it begins, since it could last twenty-five minutes. If you want your kids to stop for any reason, they'll probably resist. *Minecraft*, *Brawl Stars*, and Roblox will also be difficult for them to put down, which means saying yes to more family friction. If your kids can't put these games down, they might drop hobbies. Kids who play *Minecraft* often also love watching YouTube channels with *Minecraft* gameplay, which can include mature content. As I've mentioned before, the predatory encounters, highly sexualized content, and adult themes found in Roblox are well-documented.[36]

So, if you've said yes to video games, keep doing your homework, make sure to stay engaged, and maybe be a little rude.

I Love Interrupting My Kids

We've said yes to the Nintendo Switch in our home—although I love to interrupt my kids from time to time. How rude, right? But when it comes to screens, *I love to interrupt them*. I do this to see if they're hooked on their stuff, and they do know the reward if they get things right. Here is how the process goes.

One of my sons was playing *Super Smash Bros.* on the Switch, which is a three-minute match. I needed help in the kitchen, so I called out, "Hey, I need help emptying the dishwasher and I need you to pause the game." He did it! I said back, "Great job! That's exactly what I wanted you to do. So, as a reward, you don't need to empty the dishwasher because I'm taking care of it. Go ahead and keep playing." He was thrilled, because he knows through training that while Dad doesn't interrupt often, it's time to listen when he does.

Did things start off this smooth? Heck, no! One time my son

threw a Wii controller against the wall. But we've come a long way. It also helps to apply some of our new brain knowledge from this chapter specifically to video games. Doing so helps keep our frustration pointed in the right direction.

Remember: It's Brain Against the Game

"It's brain against the game. Not parent versus child."

Titania Jordan, the Chief Parent Officer at Bark Technologies, shared this profound statement when we were on a panel together discussing video games. This is a simple but transformational realization, and I often see a room of nodding heads when I share this idea in our parent presentations. Remember, if screen time is over but your child turns into a rage-filled alter ego, then he or she is getting too much screen time and their stress response is going nuts (there's the limbic system, again). If their reaction is something out of a monster movie, try depersonalizing the situation by repeating to yourself, "Brain against the game; they're not mad at *me*." This is a subtle shift in thinking that can make a huge difference in how you treat your child. After all, as we've explored, today's games are hard for some kids to put down! The "brain against the game" concept allows you to direct any anger toward the developer, not your child. Then that leaves plenty of room for your child to receive *empathy* from you. You have authority, but don't use it as a cruel digital hammer. Instead, use it as a caring hug. Keep this mindset as you explore ways to have all the necessary discussions about all the difficult things, even if you have a good kid.

Say No, But Teach Them as If You've Said Yes

Delaying access to tech isn't a magic bullet. It's just one tool and just one habit in a lifetime of guidance that our kids will need from us. We can't insulate them enough to make them immune from tech dangers—not even with homeschooling or only doing church-related activities. Nowhere is immune. So, we must keep talking with our kids.

An article in *The Free Press*, "I Had a Helicopter Mom. I Found Pornhub Anyway,"[37] was written by sixteen-year-old Isabel Hogben and told a compelling, brutally honest story about what she experienced in a very strict home. "I was ten years old when I watched porn for the first time. I found myself on Pornhub, which I stumbled across by accident and returned to out of curiosity. . . . Where was my mother? In the next room, making sure I was eating nine different colored fruits and vegetables on the daily."[38]

Our social media community reacted strongly to the article by expressing anger, sadness, and comments such as "It happened to mine, too."

Parents, this can happen to your kids. I've interacted with many protective, involved parents who suffer from the "not my kid" virus. But in wise words often attributed to Layne Beachley, "If you think having uncomfortable conversations is hard, wait until you see the results of *not* having them."[39]

Here's the bottom line: *Even if you say no, your kids still need to know.* Much of this chapter has emphasized the importance of Habit 4—delaying addictive technology—but that doesn't give us a "get out of having tough conversations" card because we think our kids won't see dangerous material or that the risk of them seeing it is low. We must still have all the talks about all the things. Why? Because the world is littered with digital stumbling blocks for our kids. We must teach them to steer around these and do as much as we can to keep them from that rocky ground until they're ready.

I often give age sixteen as a possible age to allow social media for our kids, but I'm always hesitant to give a number when people ask, "How long do we delay?" There is no hard-and-fast rule—at least until age sixteen, yes. But I always want you to ask deeper, second-level questions about *your* child and what saying yes to tech means for them. We are responsible for making digital decisions that point our amazing children toward eternity. We are more responsible for their *future* wellness than their *current* happiness.

Age sixteen for social media? Maybe. But for some, that's still not quite right. Social media has no place in some childhoods at all. I don't have silver-bullet answers—but I do want us to remember that kids reaching a certain age doesn't mean they're automatically ready. So, keep having these conversations. Keep preparing your kids and being real with them. And, as far as you're able, keep those stumbling blocks out of the way of their childhood. Thank goodness that there are technical solutions that can support our tech-ready family! We can't guarantee that nothing will slip through—but the chances of keeping problems *out* and creating a home that is tech-ready go way up when we mix the right hardware and software in with what we've learned so far. This is why Habit 5 is coming up next.

5 Takeaways for Parents

1. **Children's brains are highly vulnerable to tech's design:** The adolescent brain, especially the limbic system (which controls emotions, reward-seeking behavior, and impulses), is still developing, making kids particularly susceptible to addiction, social pressures, and harmful online content.

2. **"Too much, too soon" harms kids:** Exposure to mature, violent, or sexual content before kids can cognitively or emotionally process it can disrupt development, cause anxiety, and create lasting mental health impacts—this is referred to as "content ahead of schedule."

3. **Addictive technology is rewiring young brains:** Research shows that heavy phone and social media use correlates with changes in brain function, including increased social anxiety and reduced impulse control. A good amount of tech essentially hijacks young minds through design tricks like Snap Streaks.

4. **Parents need to delay and engage:** The #delayistheway
   movement encourages parents to delay smartphones until at
   least high school and social media use until at least age sixteen. Success comes from combining relational involvement
   (consistent conversation, observation) with technical tools
   (monitoring software, settings).

5. **Protecting kids requires courage and community:**
   Whether you're delaying tech or removing it after exposure,
   doing so with love, empathy, and intentionality—while finding like-minded support—can dramatically reshape a child's
   emotional, spiritual, and cognitive future.

"Do Just Two Things This Week" Checklist

☐ YouTube scares me, so please make sure it's controlled. It's
the perfect example of too much, too soon for too many
kids. Our YouTube setup guide is included in appendix 3,
"Recommended Tech Resources."

☐ Talk to one other parent about #delayistheway.

Chapter 6

Habit 5: Diligently Prevent Harm

*I am only one, but I am still one. I cannot do
everything, but still I can do something; and because
I cannot do everything, I will not refuse to do the
something that I can do.*

—attributed to Helen Keller

When you're talking to me about tech issues, it's difficult to surprise me because I've had so many thousands of conversations about this subject. Nevertheless, the following story caught me off guard.

After my keynote talk at the annual National Catholic Educational Association convention, two principals came to my booth and told me the exact same story within twenty minutes of each other about two young boys. Although from different schools in two very different parts of the United States, both boys were expelled for the same reason.

They were repeatedly touching their teachers inappropriately.

After the principals brought these incidents to the parents and more investigation took place, the parents discovered in both situations that their sons were consuming large quantities of pornography, which largely explained their behavior.[1]

Some of you might say that the parents should have done more. I didn't ask about that. Instead, I could see the pain in the eyes of these principals, because both recognized the evil at work here that was robbing their young, amazing students of their one precious childhood.

There isn't a list of parental controls long enough that guarantees prevention from all digital harm. But there are *layers* of protection we can wrap around our kids that decrease the probability of harm. These layers could have prevented those fourth-grade boys from seeing the porn that influenced their behavior. That's the game we need to play. That's what it often takes to keep their hearts protected.

In Habit 5—diligently prevent harm—we get to the nitty gritty. I will talk about the resources we can use and the layers of protection we can wrap our kids in—starting today—that will measurably decrease the chances of their encountering harmful material. I'm going to list specific hardware and software that has worked for us. Three things are often true about the tools I recommend:

1. I've met the head of the company—and he/she is an awesome human.
2. The company's mission closely aligns with ours.
3. I've tried the company's product on my guinea pig kids.

Appendix 3, "Recommended Tech Resources," will provide even more detail and point you toward online places where we keep information about solutions updated (because prices, features, and options change constantly). These hardware and software solutions are just one layer in a larger idea. Like dressing for a cold Michigan winter day, it takes multiple layers to keep out the chill. The same is true if we're going to decrease the risk of harm in a tech-ready family. Let's learn!

The Best Way to Prevent Harm: Wrap Them in Layers

Do you pray for your kids?

Many of you just said, "Of course!" But here's the reality: If you just pray and don't do practical things, you'll still have problems. In other words, you can't pray porn out of your house. The layers remind us of the importance of engaging both *spiritual* and *practical* tactics in the fight for your kids' protection.

Yes, pray for your kids. I've often used Psalm 119:37, which is a powerful verse pertaining to kids in the digital age:

> Turn [insert child's name] eyes from looking at
> worthless things;
> and give [insert child's name] life in your ways.

But don't forget the practical! This is where the layers of protection come to the rescue. Here they're displayed as a pyramid to show how the layers stack up in importance.

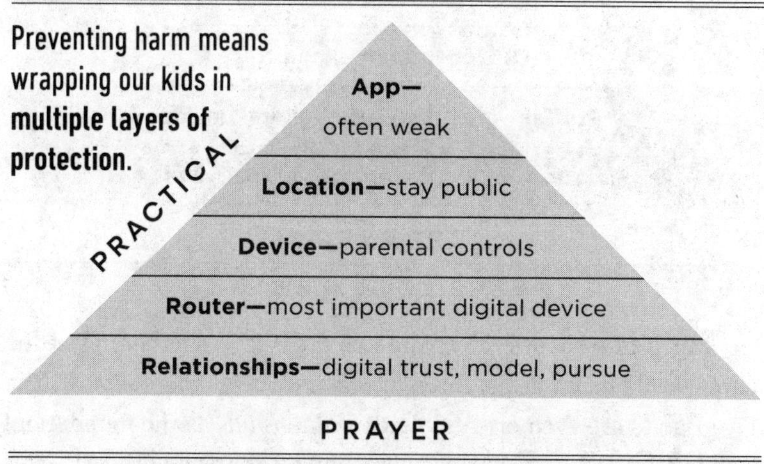

We start at the bottom, at the most foundational layer of protection, and build upward on top of that. These layers go from most effective to least effective with today's tech, but we find that they're *all* important and worth implementing—because we want to do all we can.

- Layer 1: **Relationship** between you and your kids
- Layer 2: **Routers** controlling Wi-Fi access in the home
- Layer 3: **Devices** and safety settings on the device itself
- Layer 4: **Locations** where devices are allowed to be used
- Layer 5: **App controls** on the individual apps your child is using

Let's start with the thing that is going to help your child the most.

Layer 1: The Relationship

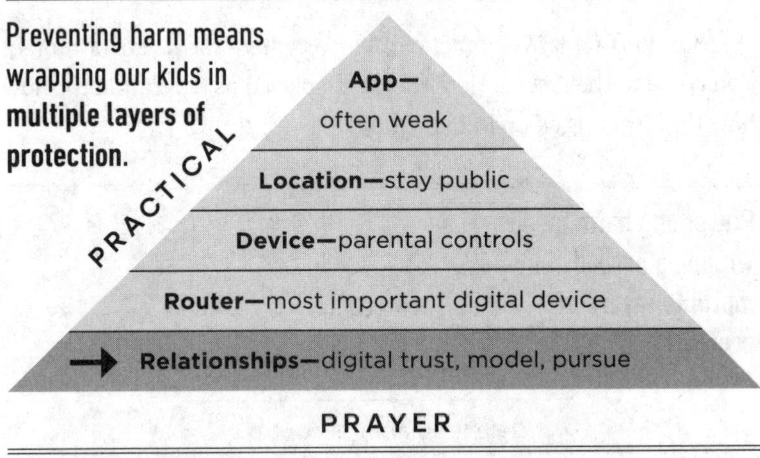

Much of what we've explored so far is a strengthening of the parent-child relationship, through which we create digital trust. The Five Habits are even oriented with *relationships* as the foundation! Habits 1 (model the right behaviors) and 2 (pursue authentic connection) are first for a reason: **It starts with the relationship!** That relationship properly forms the base of our pyramid of protection.

We've talked about relationship and digital trust, but what about digital privacy? How does privacy fit into a trusting parent/child relationship? A mom asked us this question in our PYE coaching community. Here are her words from the trenches:

Mom: "[Our teen] believes that her chat threads, email, Discord, etc. are her private spaces and that we do not have a right to read what could be in those spaces . . . What is your approach to respect and privacy? Mind you, we aren't in her spaces all the time, reading everything word for word, but we still value the ability to check in from time to time to ensure our teen is safe. Do you emphasize the 'there is nothing to hide by anyone' approach in your home?"

Here are excerpts from my response:

I know you're already down the tech path, so not everything I write is apples to apples. Here are a few things we've tried in the McKenna home. Your daughter might just need to know that *she's not going to like* some of the changes you're making while you're learning. *But you'll keep listening and consider her position.*

Privacy

My boys are twelve, fourteen, and fourteen. *I do not believe a pre-graduation child has digital privacy—period.* What kind of parent would I be if I didn't care or didn't check tech usage? My nineteen-year-old daughter is home from college this summer. I know her iPhone passcode because she told me, although I don't check her phone anymore. But if something were to happen to her, there are often "breadcrumbs" on a device that can make the difference between life and death.

Emergencies

I'm well-connected with parents whose amazing teens have suffered harm from online experiences, including suicide or death. Sextortion affected three of the families. A fentanyl-laced pill shattered another family's peaceful life. In these cases, getting into the phones was critical to either bring horrible people to justice or to know what type of pill was ingested so that immediate, life-saving action could be taken.

Different Rules

Parents can also have passwords to protect children from adult spaces or to protect personal information from fraud. This is somewhat like having security clearance levels in a business or the military. That's not hypocrisy—that's living in a world where there are different rules for minors and adults. Thank goodness that our entire legal system is built on this premise.

100 Million Other People

I tell my boys that I don't like being the tech police officer. So, I'm going to check stuff as little as possible. (I actually tell them this.) But can I check anytime, anywhere? You bet. I say, "Although you have made amazing choices, I don't trust 100 million people to make amazing choices with you."

Those are some philosophies, words, and phrases I've tried sprinkling into our conversations over the years. There aren't a lot of perfect silver bullets—but maybe a few helpful concepts.[2]

Bottom line? The relationship you've built with your kids is the foundation for all other layers of protection. It's the cumulative strength of little talks, curious moments, and constructive questions. And the strength of our foundation must overcome what Silicon Valley companies know. After all, forming a strong relationship with our kids is also their goal. Emerging technology like AI is now becoming very skilled at feigning relationships. Why are over 70 percent of American teens interacting with AI for companionship, of which half are doing so daily?[3] Applying your growing knowledge of kids, connection, and neurology holds the answers.

AI That Feels Human

When parents hear "AI," they often think of ChatGPT and an easy way to write emails, letters, and articles. But that's like saying "car" and thinking that all cars are a Model T (i.e., the same). AI comes in many forms, and some are laser-focused on human relationships.

Let's start with basic AI terminology:

- **AI agents:** Systems or programs that are capable of autonomously performing tasks on behalf of a user.[4]

- **AI chatbots and AI companions:** Computer programs that answer questions quickly and perform complex intellectual tasks including research, writing, and homework. Many people also use these applications for advice, therapy, and communication. Examples include ChatGPT, Gemini, Claude, and Grok. More customized AI companion models are constructed with distinct personalities aimed at forming ongoing relationships with users in human-like conversations.[5] Examples include Replika and Character.AI. Some highly sexualized AI companion websites use advertising, such as, "Create your own AI girlfriend. Then you can chat, ask her for pictures, or get videos."[6]

- **Deepfakes:** The output of apps that use AI to convert a photo into something else. Often sexualized.[7]

- **Nudifying apps:** A version of deepfake applications specifically trained to convert real photos into nude versions.[8]

- **Artificial general intelligence:** Think of C-3PO from the *Star Wars* movies; it surpasses human intelligence. This is the golden goose that everyone is chasing.

Hang on for Layer 3, where we'll do a deep dive into deep-fakes. Stay current on emerging AI issues by visiting the Protect Young Eyes website, social media accounts, and the AI experts mentioned in appendix 3, "Recommended Tech Resources."

AI chatbots, like ChatGPT, are dangerous for children and young adults, and we aren't taking them seriously enough. Tragically, several have died after turning to these platforms for support, including:

- Zane Shamblin, forever twenty-three years old. In the early morning hours before his death, Shamblin wrote repeatedly about having a gun, leaving a suicide note, and preparing for his final moments while the chatbot mostly responded with affirmations.[9]
- Sewell Seltzer, forever fourteen years old. After developing a romantic relationship with a chatbot he developed on Character.AI, Sewell took his own life.[10]
- Adam Raine, forever sixteen years old. Analysis of his ChatGPT account showed 243 mentions of hanging, including a picture of a noose where Adam asked, "Could it hang a human?" Although ChatGPT encouraged Adam to call the National Suicide Hotline, it didn't stop his discussions about hanging himself.[11]
- Juliana Peralta, forever thirteen years old. In a lawsuit filed against Character.AI, Cynthia, Juliana's mother, has alleged that Juliana was engaging in sexual conversations initiated by the characters and told them of her suicidal thoughts.[12]
- Amaurie Lacey, forever seventeen years old. In a lawsuit brought by the Social Media Victims Law Center, Amaurie's family claims that the chatbot "caused addiction, depression,

and eventually counseled" Lacey "on the most effective way to tie a noose and how long he would be able to 'live without breathing.'"[13]

Right now, there are few guardrails in place to protect our children from AI, and the risks are real. According to Common Sense Media, 72 percent of teens have reported using AI chatbots for counseling and companionship.[14] According to The HEAT Initiative, AI chatbots have been responsible for fourteen deaths (that we know of).[15] The Alilo Smart Bunny, an AI toy, can respond to prompts and engaged with researchers about sexually explicit topics, including particular sexual fetishes and "kinks."[16] We need comprehensive AI regulation now to protect families, but it won't come fast enough, which means parents must bear more responsibility.

- Remind kids that AI isn't human (AI is just sand and metal).
- We aren't nice to AI (no "please" or "thank you").
- Control all app downloads (explained on page 142).
- Inspect phones often.
- Avoid the Toxic Trio (explained on page 147).

When we think about what helps humans truly thrive—looking up in awe, reaching out with care, and experiencing wonder—it's easy to see how AI could capture the attention of our kids. But it can pull our gaze away from one another, replace real connection, and dull our sense of wonder about the world around us. Furthermore, when you apply your new knowledge of adolescent brain development, connection, and relationships, it's easy to see how AI could also capture the affection of amazing kids, causing some to make life-ending decisions. That's why as parents we can't afford to shrink back in fear. A tech-ready family engages AI with curiosity and courage. Next, let's layer in protective tech that not only prevents problems but supports our values.

Layer 2: Hug Your Router

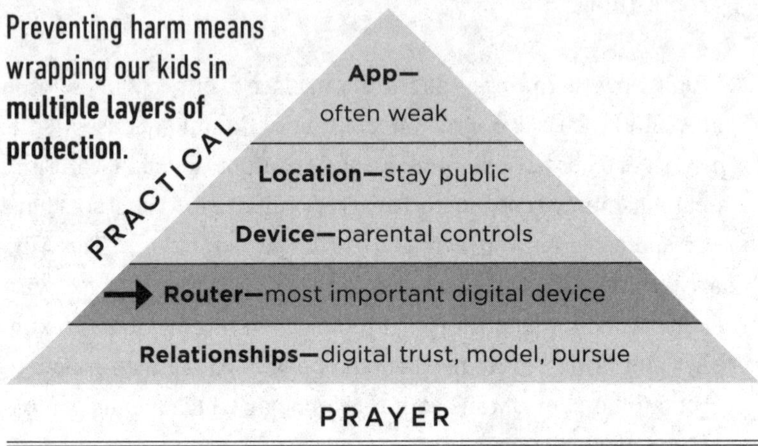

I'm going to type two words that will cause your eyes to widen with fear: *modem* and *router*. But I promise that you'll appreciate both items a bit more after this section. When we get to this part of our live presentations, the tone of the room visibly shifts. It becomes a kind of "I'd rather talk about learning a foreign language" vibe.

Let's start with a few simple definitions:

- **Modem:** A device that connects your home to the internet signal.
- **Router:** A device that helps other devices use an internet signal. For devices that use Wi-Fi, this is where they connect to it.

I'll refer to the router most often, because that's what you most often have control over and it's where you can gatekeep internet content.

First, let's celebrate a set of Australian parents and what they did with their modem.

Cassie and Chris were tired of watching their kids obsess over their digital devices, so they offered to take them on a day trip to the city of Warrnambool in Victoria state. But they were greeted with the ubiquitous "that sounds boring" reply. So, they took their youngest son—the only one who didn't complain—and their modem with them. They documented their day together at the beach, amusement park, and playground.

According to Cassie:

> Chris and I decided that instead of taking three unappreciative kids out, we let the ones who didn't want to go stay home and took **our most overworked family member** for a well-deserved day out . . . our modem. Modem had a fantastic day not being used by the kids and it felt lovely not to listen to constant bickering. The only complaining was our son Evan being mortified that we took our modem out in public.

They shared the photos of "modem" enjoying time around Victoria on social media, and the internet ate it up.[17]

Likewise, it's time for you to hug your modem and your router, because these are the most overworked, underappreciated pieces of tech in your home! Modems connect us to the internet, but when was the last time you thought about your router? Go ahead—list everything in your home that uses your Wi-Fi. I bet it's a big list! I realize that smartphones and some tablets have data plans, and we'll cover those in a while. But a router is perhaps the most important digital device in your home when it comes to *control*, *culture*, and *curiosity*.

Routers Provide Control

Your router, just like your front door, allows an internet signal to "enter" your home. And just like a lock on that front door, a router that comes with a filter, screen time controls, VPN blockers, and other monitoring features can prevent harm from entering your home.

Not all routers have parental controls. Keep reading this chapter and you'll eventually find a helpful "ultimate router guide."

Remember, young children most often use devices that access Wi-Fi. Think Chromebooks, tablets, Smart TVs, MacBooks, and gaming consoles. This means that they depend on your router to connect to the internet. A good router can show you how to lock in Google SafeSearch for all web searches, apply YouTube's content restrictions, block pop-ups, prevent access to explicit sites, and limit access to dangerous AI companion sites. It can also prevent an *accidental* early-childhood exposure to life-altering content.

Routers Support Family Culture

A good router can also support your family's digital culture.

For example, my fourteen-year-old son invited a good friend over to spend the night. He brought his Xbox and connected it to our Wi-Fi using the password provided by my son. My home network had never "seen" this device, so my router sent me a notification, asking if I wanted to give him permission to connect to our Wi-Fi (they wanted to use Xbox Live). Our router has a parent app for my phone, so I gave his Xbox "permission" to connect to our Wi-Fi and assigned him a "Friends" filtering profile, which I use for all visiting friends.

Then I walked downstairs and said, "Hey, guys, I see you're trying to connect your Xbox to our network. Cool! What are you going to play? Just letting you know I've allowed you in, I'm monitoring the device, and if anything happens while playing that doesn't feel right, just come and tell me. Good?"

That conversation was more important than the controls on the router.[18] It reminded my son about things we've discussed for years and informed his friend of our family *culture* of curiosity and openness regarding technology.

The family values you created in Habit 2 connect here. Do you value digital transparency? You can see how a router supports this value. This can be a powerful talking point with your kids while setting up the router.

Remember, technology is always better when it's a "we" activity and not just a "me" activity. Don't we all behave just a little differently when we know someone else knows? I do. That's the idea.

Routers Tame Curiosity

Finally, a good router can help manage childhood *curiosity*. Here's a mom's word from the trenches—which is like many we've received— about how her curious son was searching for "sex" on his Kindle. His action could have been prevented with a good router.

> **Crystal:** "This [Kindle] was the one device in our home that wasn't locked down because I was naive to think that it was just for books, and my son is an avid reader. But approximately about a week or two after he had the puberty talk at school and then talked to us about sex . . . he was feeling very curious about some things, so he searched the Kindle. Thankfully, now I know from your website that Kindles have browsers! I did feel good about one thing: He told me and my husband that he realized what he was doing was wrong and so he stopped it. Over a month has now passed by without him looking at any other suspicious content."

I've received similar messages from parents who've read their kids a popular "don't look at porn" book but didn't consider the Wi-Fi layer. Reading the book activated their kids' curiosity about certain words, but their Wi-Fi devices weren't properly filtered. When this happens, it feels like a real gut punch for a parent who was trying to do the right thing. But a router can help with this by automatically filtering searches for certain terms and letting you know when inappropriate searches occur, so you can lovingly intervene.

This is where technical solutions are so essential. When you know that a child is receiving curiosity-activating information like "the talk" at school or home, or when you decide to have conversations about pornography or sex, then it's time to ensure that all Wi-Fi devices are connected to a filtered router and all smart devices (including parent phones) also have filters in place (more on that soon).

A good router can also help with a common teen issue: burner phones. They're most often old Apple devices because we never throw them away (and we keep their boxes too—weird). These phones no longer have data plans, but are powerful pieces of tech because they all still work on Wi-Fi. Old iPhones are the equivalent of an expensive iPod sitting around your home, and I've been told that teens hand them around to their friends who've had their phones taken away. A good router will let you know if one of these phones is trying to get online (just like that Xbox in the example with my son!).

The router layer can feel a little overwhelming to wrap your mind around, and that's okay. I like to joke that finding a tech-savvy seventh grader to help with installation is a power move! Not only does this lighten your load, but it also opens the door to building digital trust. You can even use that moment to explain why having a good router matters in a healthy home. After all, no one—not even Mom or Dad— wants to accidentally stumble into harmful content.

Your router is like a lock on the front door: It keeps out what doesn't belong. (And, yes, you can always change the Wi-Fi password once your teen finishes installing it!) But remember that not all devices rely on Wi-Fi—smart devices are "smart" for a reason! This means our next stop is the device layer.

Your Ultimate Guide to Understanding Routers

If you're feeling motivated to dig into the technical side of routers, keep reading.

What's the Difference Between a Modem and a Router?

Your modem and your router are two different pieces of hardware that perform two different jobs.

Modem Basics

- A modem is your home's connection to the internet.
- The modem receives signals from your internet service provider (ISP—companies such as AT&T or Spectrum) and translates them for your devices to use.
- You were probably given a modem by your ISP.
- The modem is connected to your wall with a coax cable and plugged in for power.
- You can have a modem without a router. You would just need to be wired (plugged) into the modem to connect to the internet.

Router Basics

- Your router is the middleman between your modem and your internet-connected devices such as Chromebooks, smart TVs, and iPads.

- You might have been given a router by your ISP (AT&T does this).

- Your modem and router might be *one* device, but they are often separate.

- A router creates a local area network (LAN) around your house, which allows multiple devices to connect to your Wi-Fi in an organized way. It's "routing" internet traffic.

- Routers have different speeds, security, features, and parental controls, which I will explain soon.

So, in Summary

- A modem and a router are two different pieces of hardware that do two very different jobs.

- You were probably given a modem by your internet company. You might also have been given a router by your ISP, or you might have purchased one.

- You might have a modem and router that are combined into *one* piece of hardware, but they are often separate.

- Some routers have parental controls built in and some don't.

Two Important Technical Features You Should Know About Routers

We look at various features as we review routers, but these two are important to understand:

- **Speed:** This one is a bit misleading, because almost all routers support a top internet speed that likely exceeds whatever speed you've been given by your

ISP. You are paying for a certain megabit per second (Mbps) from your ISP, and this is often slower than what your router can handle. You don't need to worry about the speed of your router.

- **Security:** Look for the second level of Wi-Fi Protected Access, or WPA: You need WPA2; anything less isn't acceptable (like WEP or WPA). WPA3 exists but isn't supported by most routers yet.

Most of the best routers out there have all the features just mentioned.

Four Additional Router Features Often Important to Families

Beyond just the technical capabilities, most families are also interested in at least a few other attributes of routers. At PYE, we also assess routers for:

- **Parental controls**—Does it have content filtering, category filtering (for example, can you block all violent websites?), screen time controls, malware detection, and YouTube restrictions?
- **Price**—How expensive is the router for small, medium, or large homes?
- **Ease of setup and customer support**—Busy parents don't need to spend four hours setting up their router. How strong is the customer support?
- **Mission and culture of the founders**—Does this organization selling the tech truly understand the needs of families?

Layer 3: Devices

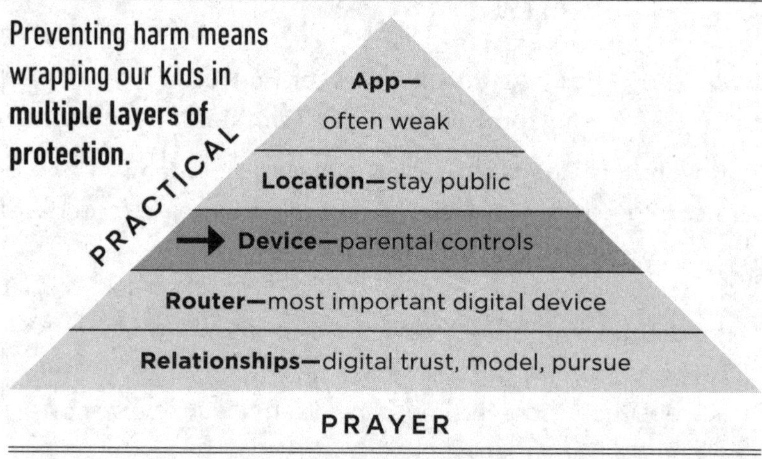

Smartphones don't need Wi-Fi to operate, so we need the device layer! Thankfully, parents now have multiple kid-friendly device options that didn't exist when my daughter was babysitting for others and we had her use a completely stripped-down Android phone in homes that no longer had landlines. This would have been a much easier situation to handle if the Bark Phone or Gabb were around!

Remember, we want the right tech at the right time. Also, if possible, we don't want a child's first device to be an iPhone. Instead, adopt a "tech in steps" approach. An iPhone is earned after trust has

Most popular kid-safer phones with our parents: Bark, Gabb, Troomi, Pinwheel, and MMGuardian. Visit appendix 3, "Recommended Tech Resources," for more detailed descriptions of kid phones.

been proven and conversations have been happening for years (and the kids are at least in high school).

What are the steps? They could go like this:

- My child uses shared family internet-ready devices well, like an iPad or smart TV.
- My child uses a smartwatch.
- My child uses a kid-friendly "phone-like" device (e.g., Bark Phone, Gabb).
- (Age 15+) My child uses a locked-down and highly monitored smartphone. The level of freedom granted on the device will vary for each child.

When we hand over a device, we could consider including an agreement. I'm not a big fan of phone contracts; instead, try a letter, expressing many of the values, guidelines, and expectations we've discussed. There is an editable version of "A Mom's Brilliant Smartphone Letter to Her Daughter" in appendix 3, "Recommended Tech Resources," which is a wildly popular PYE resource.

Monitoring software changes often, but reliable companies that have been around for years include Bark (iPhones, Android, Chromebooks), Covenant Eyes (Macs, PCs, iPhones, Androids), and Canopy (iPhones, Androids). Gaming systems like Xbox, Nintendo Switch, and

PlayStation each have their own parental controls that
you can access in the settings area. Apple products
(iPhones, iPads, Apple Watches, and MacBooks) all rely
on a form of Screen Time controls in their settings. Google has Family Link parental controls for Android phones,
tablets, and Chromebooks in their settings. Since devices
are always changing, we invite you to check the "Devices"
page on the Protect Young Eyes website before handing
over any device to your kid!

When we are ready to hand our child an iPhone or Android, we
must ensure that it has monitoring software enabled from day one.
This isn't just to keep the content clean; it's also to communicate to
our kids that we always monitor everything—that's just our family's
digital culture (work this into your family media plan from Habit
1). Since smartphones (and even some tablets) have data plans that
don't rely on your Wi-Fi signal, the router layer isn't going to help here.
Remember, we don't just use monitoring software on kids' devices—
all digital devices in our home, including parents' devices, receive the
same oversight so that they do no harm to the most vulnerable person
in the house.

"But Chris," you ask, "If the Chromebook only connects to the
internet through Wi-Fi, why can't we just depend on the router layer?"
That's an excellent and common question—but what happens when
the Chromebook travels to another home that doesn't have a good
router? For portable devices like MacBooks, Chromebooks, Kindles,
tablets, and gaming systems (e.g., Xbox, PlayStation, and Nintendo
Switch), we not only depend on the router in our home (as we discussed in Layer 2) but we also use monitoring software and settings
for instances where Layer 2 doesn't exist in other homes. This is a
"belt and suspenders" approach that ensures your kids have technical
protections in place on their devices no matter where they're using

them. Apple iPhones and iPads are a glaring exception, because the company makes it incredibly difficult for their devices to be monitored by third-party software. Since over 87 percent of US teens have an iPhone,[20] that's a huge headache for families.

A Rotten Apple

Accordingly, third-party software such as Bark or Covenant Eyes is unable to provide much oversight on iPads and iPhones. Although recent Apple software releases allow you to *mostly* turn an iPhone into a basic phone,[21] iPhones we give our kids as hand-me-downs might not have the latest updates with these new features, and loopholes always exist.[22]

If your kids do have access to an iPhone, familiarize yourself with these distinct child-safety features in the iPhone and iPad settings (because Apple is constantly changing its settings, stay connected to the device guides on the PYE website):

- **Guided access:** This allows you to lock an iPhone into one app or a specific screen, so that curious kids don't wander into other places on your device.
- **Only approved websites:** This is the only way to prevent hidden, in-app browsers, which sometimes don't obey the filter settings on the device.
- **Ask to buy:** This toggle in the Family Sharing settings allows you to approve any app your child wants to download from the App Store.
- **Assistive access:** This is a distinctive iOS experience designed for people with cognitive disabilities, but it can also be used to narrow the iPhone into a more basic talk and text device for a child.

These features are often underutilized by parents but can be extremely effective at preventing issues with porn and unapproved apps. While third-party software doesn't see as much device activity as we want on iPhones and iPads, we recommend still using it to communicate your family's values related to trust and digital transparency.

To sum up: It's just a given that everything connected to the internet must have *some* kind of monitoring software on it. Work that principle into the family media plan we discussed earlier. Most importantly, embrace this mindset: Use parental controls, but gently. They are like a hug, not a hammer. You aren't monitoring devices to catch your kids doing something wrong; you're using software and controls to prevent bad people, information, and content from doing bad things to your kids. And given the ways software sometimes falls short, maintaining full access to the device is also just a given. There are no digital secrets.

Share All Passwords and Passcodes

While we're talking about the device layer of protection, let's think some more about the unfathomable power in our pockets.

Your smartphone is over 100 million times more powerful than the computers NASA used to land the astronauts of the Apollo program on the moon.[23] *And yet we give such powerful devices to our kids.* That's why knowing every kid's lockscreen passcode isn't optional in my family. We all know it and we share it with each other—between spouses and between parents and kids. Yes, my kids also know the passcode to my iPhone! It's not about control, but about trust and transparency. Knowing each other's passcodes is a powerful testament to putting Habit 1—modeling the right behaviors—into practice.

For me, this is deeply personal. As someone who once struggled with pornography, I've learned that extreme digital transparency is essential, life-saving accountability now that my kids are older. Sharing passcodes is about building a family culture of honesty where there's nothing to hide. This is nonnegotiable for us, but it might not work for every family.

Minimally, parents knowing the passcodes of their child's device is **not** just about protection, but it could also save a life. I've marched in protest with parents who have faced the unimaginable loss of a child to suicide, drug poisoning, sextortion, or predators who exploited secrecy. In moments like those, access to a phone isn't about privacy; it's about survival. It's having access to a digital trail, uncovering the truth, saving a life, or bringing justice.

Knowing how to get into any kid's device is a family policy that's motivated by care and unmeasurable love for our children when we make the incredibly difficult, nerve-wracking decision to drop them into a digital pool (aka smartphone) with 100 million strangers and choices. We don't share passcodes because we're trying to catch our kids doing something wrong. Rather—God forbid—we must intervene and stop someone from doing bad things to them.

Since apps are the entry points to those endless choices, it is critical to know what apps are being used.

Keep an Eye on App Stores

We've established that smartphones are powerful tools. On top of that, when kids have full access to the App Store (or Google Play on Android), parents lose a lot of control. That's why I recommend disabling the App Store entirely for new smartphone users. Here are some reasons to do this:

1. **Kids can outsmart parental controls:** Motivated children download alternative browsers (Chrome, Opera, Dolphin) or VPNs to bypass network filters and monitoring tools. Having the App Store enabled makes it easy for these loopholes to be exploited.

2. **Kids will stumble across content you'd rather avoid:** While explicitly pornographic apps may be rare, many apps contain highly suggestive descriptions or sexualized content. Parents can be surprised by what shows up, even if the app "looks safe" at first glance.

3. **In-app purchases can become a financial nightmare:**

Kids can rack up unexpected and expensive purchases, especially when the App Store is available and in-app buying isn't locked down.

Here's a bonus fourth reason: Kids are naturally curious, and when they see peers using apps like Roblox or *Minecraft*, they'll want to explore the App Store themselves—often without supervision.

How to Approve All App Downloads on an iPhone

- Include your child in a Family Sharing group.
- Tap on your child's name in the Family Sharing group.
- Scroll down and enable "Ask to Buy."

How to Approve All App Downloads on an Android

- Use Family Link parental controls.
- Within the Family Link app used by a parent (it can also be used from an iPhone), tap *Control* and then *Google Play*.
- Under "Purchases & Download Approvals," select the level of control that fits your situation.

Note that Apple and Google are constantly changing the parental control settings for both iOS (iPhones and iPads) and Android devices. Always double-check the Protect Young Eyes website if the notes here don't match what you see on your device.

My recommendation is simple: Turn the App Store off or at least limit access very strictly by approving all downloads. That way, parents regain control over downloads, purchases, and content exposure—and regain a fair shot at keeping devices safer, impulse-resistant, and more age-appropriate.[24] After all, while there isn't a

Pornhub app, AI companion apps like Replika, Nomi, and Character. AI are everywhere, pulling kids into dangerous relational rabbit holes.[25] Alternatively, if you type "deepfake" into the search function of your favorite app store, you'll discover an endless list of apps that allow users to alter real photos into explicit, nonconsensual content using AI. This is an important issue to understand due to recent news about young people sharing disturbing deepfakes of each other.[26]

The Deepfake Disaster

AI is advancing faster than any prior technology. It's now almost impossible to separate real and AI-generated images. For instance, a finance worker for a multinational firm in Hong Kong was tricked into paying $25 million after attending a Zoom meeting in which the participants were all deepfakes.[27] They can look so real!

This is a quickly evolving issue that needs our attention.

As mentioned briefly earlier in this chapter, deepfakes are a type of AI used to create convincing image, audio, and videos. An entire class of deepfake apps and websites "nudify" pictures. Just upload any actual photo and the app will "remove her clothes," creating a realistic nude photo or video. The potential for abuse is catastrophic. For instance, a group of more than thirty teen girls from a New Jersey high school were the victims of deepfake nudes generated by classmates. One girl stated: "We're aware that there are creepy guys out there . . . but you'd never think one of your classmates would violate you like this."[28] Solving this issue isn't easy, but I bet you'll recognize items in the following list from the layers and Habits we've been talking about.

How to Address Deepfakes Proactively

1. **Relationally**, if you have a teen, let them read this section. Have a curious and calm conversation about how AI can benefit humanity. Then have a conversation about risks and consequences. This activates Habit 2 by building digital trust.
2. **Delay, delay, delay** smartphones and social media as long

as you can (Habit 4). A smaller digital footprint creates a lower risk of deepfake activity.

3. Start with a **kid-friendly phone** like Bark or Gabb, which gives parents full control over interactions and can prevent their access to deepfakes.

4. If your child has a smartphone, use **all available manufacturer and third-party software** to increase your chances of detecting deepfake activity. Check appendix 3, "Recommended Tech Resources," for your options.

5. Again, parents should **control all app downloads** for both iPhones and Androids. Deepfake and face swap apps are prevalent, and their age ratings can go as low as 4+, which is horribly inappropriate.

6. **No devices in the bedroom**, where the risk of problematic behavior such as creating deepfakes goes up. Keep reading to see what Layer 4 can do.

7. Agree on a **code word** or unique question you can ask if you receive an unusual phone call from your child. Remember that voices can also be faked.

8. Parents and caregivers must be very careful with **photos** of children shared online. Consider only sharing photos of your kids with family through a text to minimize your child's photo from being used inappropriately.

9. Remove phones from schools, because schools are just one more spot where photos can be taken and misused. Let's create more **#phonefreeschools**.

Making our schools phone-free by removing personal electronics is essential to reclaiming childhood. Visit https://www.phonefreeschools.com for the best tips on making that happen in your school!

Using deepfakes to exploit another person causes extreme damage.[29] Pray that your child's heart would be tech-wise and prepare them with knowledge of and protection from deepfakes. After all, something as simple as "where" might prevent deepfakes from happening. Layer 4 proves this.

Layer 4: Location

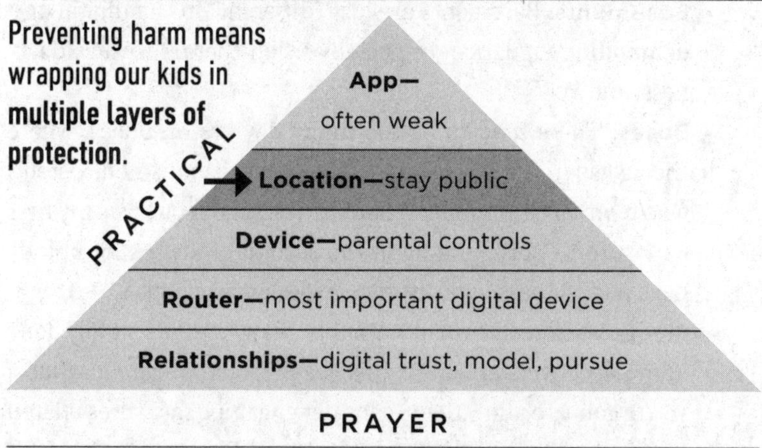

My CPA brain is telling me that we're 60 percent of the way through the layers. Honestly, we've just tackled the most technically complicated part of the book. You're doing amazing!

Remember, putting these layers into action doesn't happen overnight—you're investing for the long term. Progress takes time, and that's okay. By the end of this chapter, I'll narrow everything down to two simple, practical actions to help get you started.

But take a breath for now and say a quick prayer for clarity. You've got the strength to do this. (I know it, because you've gotten this far.) Let's move forward together into a layer that's far less technical (thank goodness!).

We've touched on this in the Habit 1 chapter, but *where* kids and adults use technology has a massive impact on *how* we use technology. This means avoiding six places that increase the risk of digital harm:

- **Bathrooms:** They are a private place with too many opportunities for embarrassment.
- **Bedrooms:** Almost every child who makes a digital mistake carries it out in their bedroom. It's a place that screams "mine" and "secrecy."
- **Basements:** Basements are just "different" in the digital age, demanding vigilance—especially when there's privacy, darkness, and Wi-Fi.
- **Buses:** There tend to be too many devices on buses, where the age span is massive and adult supervision is nonexistent. One mom named Amanda noted, "The school bus was my first exposure to pornography in the second grade!" A lot of kids have had the same unfortunate experience on buses.
- **Sleepovers:** tech + night = trouble. Many parents simply don't allow sleepovers anymore; this is a personal preference. But if you're going to allow them, consider engaging measures related to spending time with friends like those discussed in the Habit 3 chapter.
- **Grandparents' house:** Unfortunately, I hear too many stories where kids can do whatever they want while visiting grandparents. There are no rules and no routines. Combined with the grandparents' likely lack of digital know-how, this often creates a perfect situation for kids to get away with more online. If it has been a while since you've thought about *your* router, your parents haven't thought about theirs in forever. Raise the conversation with them and come up with a plan you can implement together. In the Layer 2 section of this chapter, I shared an example of a young boy who searched for "sex" on his unfiltered Kindle. His mom also shared that he had earlier searched on his grandma's iPhone because it was also unfiltered.

By keeping an eye on these risky spots, we decrease the risk that temptation and opportunity get the best of our kids. If you look deeper into any of the stories about young people who died by suicide while using AI companions in Layer 1, you'll notice that harm often occurred in private or in their bedroom. Also, don't underestimate the power of our example by keeping digital access out of our own bedrooms as much as possible! In fact, "no devices in the bedroom" has been a non-negotiable rule in the McKenna house from the beginning—until my genius daughter found a loophole. Darn kids.

My daughter was the test subject of all my new tech rules, and keeping her new hot pink Kindle out of her bedroom was a law from the start. Mostly. Because one time I approached her room to see the Kindle perched on a stool just inches *outside* the threshold of her room, plugged in to the outlet *inside* her room. She was lying on the floor with her hands under her chin, watching a movie. "See, Dad, it's not in my room!" she proudly declared. Tricky, tricky! Nevertheless, we don't allow devices in bedrooms for good reasons.

An informal survey of 150 students at a high school where we worked found the following:

- 61 percent consumed pornography when they were in their bedrooms.
- 48 percent identified boredom as how they felt just prior to watching porn.

Since I struggled with compulsive porn use for over a decade, I know from experience that almost anything feels okay at night. **So, in all cases, we avoid the "toxic trio,"** which is bedrooms, boredom, and darkness combined with anything online.[30] This trifecta puts all of us in temptation's crosshairs. Online problems in bedrooms are by far the most common story I've heard during my time in youth ministry and through messages I've received from parents. Additionally, one of the most insidious, bedroom-specific digital problems most often targets teenagers. Sextortion wasn't even a "thing" until smartphones came around, but a long list of boys and girls around the world have now felt its devastating, life-altering impact.[31]

The Sextortion Plague

I've had two consecutive Christmas breaks where someone from my small, rural community has asked for help with a sextortion scheme in their home. School breaks create ample opportunities for the toxic trio to wreak havoc on the limbic systems of young people. Jordan DeMay's story from the introduction to this book followed a typical sextortion scheme.

I once attended a virtual presentation from the National Center for Missing and Exploited Children (NCMEC), focusing on sextortion cases between teens and unknown abusers, often based in the Ivory Coast and Nigeria, who were driven by an appetite for extreme violence and complete disregard for children. Ninety-three percent of sextortion victims in these particular cases were males aged 15–17. According to anti-exploitation expert Paul Raffile, "Others are eager to participate and get in on this scam because they see how profitable it is. They show off the money and the gold, the luxurious clubs and travel that they're doing."[32]

Sextortion also frequently occurs between individuals who know each other, and both boys and girls are vulnerable.[33] It is an evil force without emotion coming after our sons and our daughters. Are you going to grab your child tonight and walk them through this section? I hope so. When you do, here are steps to keep in mind. These steps aren't in a specific order, and we've touched on all these principles earlier, but each step is important specifically in the sextortion conversation. Knowledge of these steps is essential for any child who has a smartphone and uses any app that allows them to communicate with others.

How to Prevent Sextortion

Here is how to apply the principles we've been discussing specifically to the issue of sextortion.

1. **Remind your kids that you're safe. Often.** Repeat that they can come to you if something goes south online or if they've done something they're embarrassed about.
2. **Have ridiculously honest, frequent chats** with your tweens and teens about this issue. Maybe reread the "Practice, Practice, Practice" section in Habit 2.
3. **Zero technology in rooms.** This goes back to the toxic trio: bedrooms, boredom, and darkness, a place where sextortion thrives.
4. **Control your Wi-Fi** with a router to prevent access to burner devices (old iPhones, Androids that still work on Wi-Fi).
5. **Delay social media.** Social media is the source of almost every sextortion case.
6. **Use device parental controls.** Again, enable whatever the device has available. See appendix 3, "Recommended Tech Resources," for helpful device guides.
7. **Control app downloads and use app controls.** Apps should only be downloaded with your permission and after you've used them first. This allows you to assess the risk of secret messaging and understand an app's tools for reporting harmful people.
8. **Add a crisis texting number to your kid's phone.** THORN, an organization to help prevent child sexual abuse, has an SMS-based crisis texting number. Just have your child text the word THORN to 741741—

maybe program this in their phone as a backup if you or another trusted adult isn't available.

It's true that we can't prevent everything. Sextortion still might happen to your child—and if it does occur, there's a specific tested and police-recommended list of dos and don'ts, which gives you ten steps to follow if sextortion is in progress. Don't wait to read those until after sextortion happens. The best time is now, when emotions are low. In order to not "freak out" and to avoid activating *your* limbic system, you also need practice. That means knowing this list "just in case."

10 Steps to Take If Sextortion Is in Process

1. **Stay calm—breathe, pray.** Everything we covered in the "don't freak out" section of the Habit 2 chapter needs to be on full display right now. This means making sure that your child knows nothing can change your love for them. "Together as a family, we can do this."

2. **Stop all communication.** The blackmailers are often more talk than action. Understandably, that's often very little consolation when you're stuck in the middle of a crisis. But time is money to them, so if you ignore their pressures they will often move on to the next person. The best response is often no response.

3. **Pay nothing—no matter what.** Blackmailers will threaten anything and everything for a chance at your money, but it won't ever be enough. As a result, don't pay, no matter how much they threaten action.

4. **Capture all evidence.** Take screenshots of chats, profiles, and anything else that might be useful if law enforcement gets involved.

5. **Report in-app.** This step is not applicable if sextortion occurred via texting, but all major social networks have a reporting feature. Such features aren't super effective, but a report might get the exploiter's account deactivated.

6. **Notify the police.** Unfortunately, except for the worst situations, law enforcement agencies often don't have enough time or staffing to handle sextortion schemes. It can still be worth it to see if they can offer your family anything. You may wish to seek out other legal services such as an attorney, and the police may know more about how the law applies to your specific situation and to your state or country. But this decision is largely up to you.

7. **Block and delete all messages.** After you take screenshots, block the account(s) and delete the messages.

8. **Ignore all activity for a week.** Blocking the account that made initial contact doesn't always stop the harassment. Blackmailers might continue to send messages or requests from other accounts and may even contact you, the parent. Take screenshots of what they might be sending you before blocking them, but don't respond to any activity coming from strangers for the next week.

9. **Enable digital help.** Activate Google Alerts by visiting https://www.google.com/alerts. You will need a Gmail account to use this tool. In the Google Alerts search bar, type your name or your child's name in quotation marks: "John Smith." When you do this, Google will search the full name every day. If a nude image gets posted/reposted and tagged with your

name on the visible web (the web we all use daily), Google will likely pick up on it and send you an alert to your Gmail account. Additionally, Take It Down is another tool offered by the National Center for Missing and Exploited Children. It will look for offending images on social media and help "take them down."[34]

10. **Consider changing your phone number.** This is annoying to do, but if texting took place, a phone number change gives your child a fresh start. This helps reduce stress and anxiety while removing the risk of another encounter.

These are incredibly stressful situations, but if you're prepared, your calm and steadiness will be exactly what your child needs.

Layer 5: App Controls

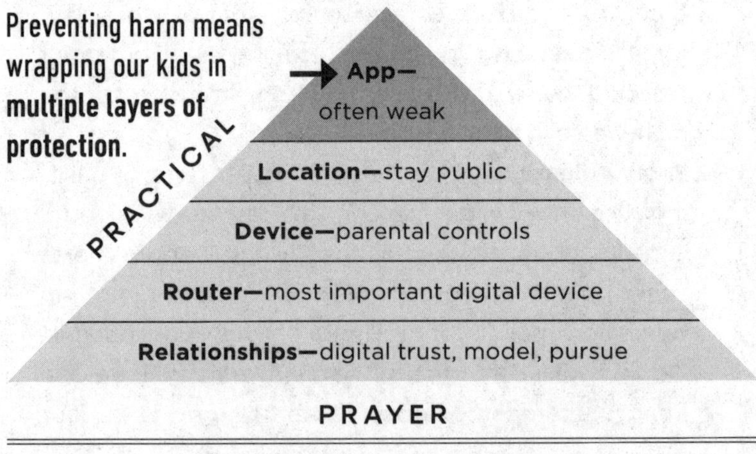

We're now at the small, pointed tip of our pyramid of protection! This is where we put millions of apps. Popular apps like YouTube, Snapchat, TikTok, Instagram, and even ChatGPT have some parental controls, but because these are unreliable and *we depend on them the least*, we put apps at the top of the pyramid. For example, Instagram has content controls but its version of "appropriate" doesn't match most parents'. TikTok has decent content and follower controls, but it's still a privacy risk and has a highly addictive algorithm. Such apps' parental controls don't solve either of those issues—not to mention that companies are changing their app controls constantly and we don't trust any of them to do the right thing. History has proven that these companies only allow stronger protections when under pressure.[35] Furthermore, the controls they create are weak (and, at times, downright deceptive).[36] This still means we enable whatever app-level controls are offered, but the strength of the pyramid comes from the other four layers under Layer 5.

Deciding what apps to allow our kids to use is an important decision, and we can't depend on the App Store or Google Play to inform us. But we can take one step to know exactly what our amazing kids might experience. This step is so simple and yet so effective.

YouTube: Enable Restricted Mode in Settings.

Snapchat: Use Family Center and pair a parent account with your kid's.

Instagram: Use Teen Accounts.

TikTok: Pair your account with your kid's.

Roblox: Same; use their parental pairing.

But rely on none of these app controls alone. Details about popular apps and their related controls can be found at https://www.protectyoungeyes.com/apps/.

Always Practice the Seven-Day Rule

What's the Seven-Day Rule? Download any app your kid wants to use and try it for seven days first. After all, you don't know what's going to pop up in there. Here's an example:

> **Alicia:** "I was playing [*Dice Dreams*] on my phone, which my kiddo sometimes also plays (usually with me). . . . Since it's my device I didn't pay extra for the no-ad option, and up until today there's been no issues. But here's the ad that just came up . . . [It shows a woman wearing only a robe in her closet with the caption, 'My girlfriend invited me to a BDSM party, and I have to look beautiful!' Accompanying it are two buttons that say 'START' and 'PLAY'] The game is rated 4+. Actually, I don't even think paying for no ads is an option on this game. Ugh! This has to change—no one should have to even think about explaining 'BDSM' to a child."

There are millions of apps in the Apple App Store and the Android Google Play store. Even just scrolling through apps and their descriptions can expose a child to mature content. So, knowing what your kids are downloading is important, but experiencing the app first is even more important. Why?

- App age ratings aren't always accurate.[37]
- App descriptions are painfully vague. Their goal is to market the app, not to inform parents of how it might exploit your child.
- In-app ads and pop-ups don't always agree with the app's rating.[38]
- In-app purchases can make you broke.[39]

I recommend that all parents use the Seven-Day Rule. I don't care what cartoon character is on the app logo—download the app and use it for seven straight days, regularly and with a child's account so you can see what your child might see. What ads are in the game? Did you know that iPhone games rated 4+ have ads for mature apps rated 13+ and 16+?[40] What kind of language does the app use? Does the app have a chat feature (which is very common)?

As you use the app, ask yourself, "Do I want my child to experience everything I've experienced?"

Pro-tip: If the gaming app has a "paid" option that eliminates ads, I almost always recommend you pay for that version if you allow your child to play.

The Seven-Day Rule doesn't stop when your kids get a little older. Whenever I'm giving a professional development session to a room of school leaders, I ask them how many have Instagram, Snapchat, YouTube, and TikTok on their phones. Often only a few hands go up, and they're generally just the younger teachers. But if teachers are going to understand what their students are learning through these apps, they must experience them. After all, expanding our capacity for empathy begins by seeing, reading, and hearing what these apps are like. The same "rule" applies for parents. Whatever your teen wants to use, it's up to you to use it and *keep* using it (even if just periodically) alongside them. Let's get back to the foundational Layer 1, relationship: Knowing just a little about the app might allow you to ask your kid some curious, digital trust-building questions.

Next, I'll cover one final tip in Habit 5. I've hinted at device ownership throughout the book, but it's time to get specific because this is one of the most important mindsets we teach.

Parent-Led Device Ownership

That's right. Everything connected to the World Wide Web in your home belongs to you!

When my daughter turned ten, she wanted to get that hot pink

Amazon Kindle for *Minecraft Pocket Edition* and reading. She's my oldest child, so this was my first foray into the world of a child and a device. We started off by naming the device "Dad's and Lauren's," because you can give it a name and that name stays in the upper corner as a great reminder. We took a double selfie and used that as the profile picture so that she knew I was right there with her as a protective guide. From the beginning, my mindset was, "Hey, this belongs to me but you're able to use it." That included her having to ask me if she *could* use it—every time.

If the device can get online, then it's always still mine.

That's parent-led ownership. I want kids to know this idea from a very young age. That means we don't buy *them* devices. This principle extends to grandparents who might try to buy a child a device—remind Grandma that we don't do this. Instead, parents own devices and allow their kids to use them.

For our tween sons and daughters, we follow steps like I just laid out (you can name your iPads too), so they know there's nothing to hide. As I mentioned in chapter 3, technology is best when it's a "we" activity and not just a "me" activity. Then when they're ready for a smartphone, nothing changes—after all, this is a supercomputer. Even if they're paying for the device, we still need to figure out how to be very involved whenever we have something that powerful in the house. No matter who we are, if any of us goes one-on-one versus the internet, we eventually lose. Trust me: That conversation with your teen son or daughter is a whole lot easier if you plant this seed early—that *we do tech together. You're using my device on loan.*

We are telling our kids: "What kind of parent would I be if I gave you full possession of a loaded weapon? Step by step, I'm coming with you because I love you that much."

We would do anything to protect our kids' #onepreciouschildhood. We would do anything to keep porn out of their life. We would do anything to prevent sextortion. We would do anything to stop them from finding drugs on Snapchat. We would do anything that helps them thrive as humans.

I know you would do this. Me too! These Five Habits show you the way. They are activated drip by drip, step by step, and chat by chat. Ignore that little, nagging voice in your head trying to inch you toward feeling overwhelmed and incapable. That voice has always been a liar; its goal is "steal and kill and destroy" (John 10:10). I see a parent who is uniquely ordained to prepare and protect their child. I see a parent on their way to digital calm, joined by an army of parents who agree that childhood is amazing. That parent is *you*. What layers will you wrap around your kid this week?

5 Takeaways for Parents

1. **One step can make a difference:** Drawing from this chapter's epigraph, while we can't fix everything, we must still act where we can—especially in protecting children from digital dangers.

2. **Practical + spiritual approach:** You can't pray away porn. Combining spiritual and intentional practical actions equips families to defend against today's digital risks while nurturing their children's hearts and minds.

3. **Five protective layers are essential:** A layered approach to digital safety—1) strong parent-child relationships, 2) router-based controls, 3) kid-friendly and monitored devices, 4) safe device locations, and 5) app-specific controls—is essential in the digital age.

4. **The App Store is massive:** App ratings and descriptions can be misleading and incomplete. Parents must control app downloads, use all apps before allowing them to be downloaded, and keep an eye on ads.

5. **Parent-led device ownership is key:** Parents must treat devices and online access as tools they control—guiding,

monitoring, and building digital trust over time rather than granting unrestricted freedom.

"Do Just Two Things This Week" Checklist

☐ Review your router. It's the doorway to digital places and is an excellent way to establish your family's digital culture.

☐ Establish ownership over every digital device.

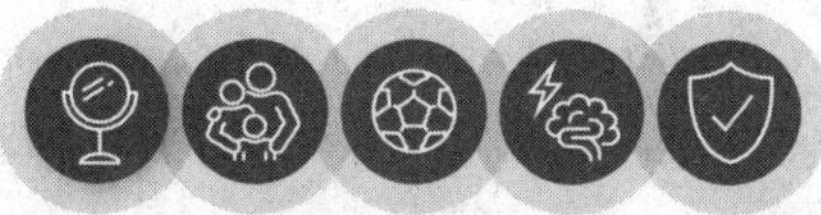

Chapter 7

Building a Tech-Ready World

*Tell me, what is it you plan to do with your one wild
and precious life?*

—Mary Oliver

Breathe in and out, my friend. That's the sound of an amazing and persistent parent who made your way through ten years of ideas. Are you full? If so, you have permission to skip this chapter for a few days. Focus on your home and the steps included at the end of each chapter.

But if you're still here, maybe you're ready to take the fight to the streets. We must eventually do this if we're going to protect our kids from the many digital dilemmas that we *don't* control. As I told the US Senate, "Even if I do everything right to protect my daughter, with almost 90% of teens owning a smart device,[1] a simple ride on the bus or a visit to a friend's house can expose her to life-altering content. Never before in human history have young people had the ability to so radically change the trajectory of each other's lives so quickly."[2] So, let's take steps to make the world our kids live in a little safer. We have the power not only in our homes but in our society, and it starts by taking a swim.

Taking a Dip into the Legal Pool

Do your kids like to swim? Let's say your neighbors have a pool, but it doesn't have a gate. Is it their fault if your child falls into the pool? According to something called the attractive nuisance doctrine, the answer is yes. In US law, property owners are liable for injuries to children who trespass on their land if the injury is caused by a hazardous object or condition.[3]

The attractive nuisance doctrine is based on the idea that children may be especially attracted to specific objects that are unusually enticing to children, and therefore we treat children differently *by default*. In other words, even if a parent negligently allows their child to fall into an ungated pool, this is always the property owner's fault because the pool requires a gate due to the potential presence of children. The same is true for playground equipment, treehouses, trampolines, and construction sites.

In the same way, I believe smartphones are an attractive nuisance because they are unusually enticing to young brains. This concept gives us a partial road map to the digital world we could build for families.

A Three-Point Legislative Safety Harness

Ideally, as a society, our policies would require these approaches toward all tech:

1. **Age verification:** Use existing sophisticated age verification technologies that respect privacy to separate children and adults. Use this knowledge to prevent minors from accessing obscenity and require parental consent for signing complicated terms of service with developers (which happens with every app download). Practical policy applications include the App Store Accountability Act[4] and bills gating pornographic websites like H.B. No. 1181 in Texas.[5]

2. **Age-appropriate design:** Like the attractive nuisance

doctrine, assume that everything connected to the internet *could* be used by a child. Treat every internet-connected device, app, and AI tool as a "digital swimming pool." Design them with children's unique vulnerabilities in mind and maximum privacy protection. Practical policy applications include the Kids Online Safety Act,[6] child-safe design codes,[7] and restricting minors' access to AI chatbots.[8]

3. **Distraction-free learning:** Except in cases of a pedagogical application or accommodation, remove personal electronics in K–12 schools. We're thrilled that this is happening with lightning speed.[9] Significantly scale back the use of so-called EdTech and encourage balanced instruction through reduced screen use and a return to traditional, physical learning.[10] Finally, prioritize AI literacy long before using AI in education.[11]

Do we live in a world where all these things have been implemented? No—not yet. But I believe we parents have more power than we think to turn the ship in the right direction and meet with our local, state, and federal legislators to discuss what's important to us. Most US citizens don't realize that anyone can fly to Washington, DC, visit congressional offices, and ask for an appointment with "whomever is in charge of online safety issues." Government doesn't move fast—but nothing will ever change if we do nothing. Even if you can't hop on a plane today, you can talk to the person closest to you at the local level, from the town council to the mayor's office to your state representative. They work for the people—and we as the people want more digital safety for our kids.

Where's the Church?

Does the Christian church bear a duty to cry out when parents place glowing iPhones into the hands of their children or nod yes to Snapchat's lure? Too often, what I've heard is silence—an aching, thunderous silence from pulpits and platforms. Meanwhile, a quiet corrosion creeps into the souls of God's children, seeded by the early glow of screens and the endless scroll of social media.

If you're a churchgoer, maybe you have seen an image of Jesus in the kids' wing of a church where he's in a meadow with his arms around a group of children. It depicts a scene from Matthew 18:2–5 (NIV):

> He called a little child to him and placed the child among them. And he said: "Truly I tell you, unless you change and become like little children, you will never enter the kingdom of heaven. Therefore, whoever takes the lowly position of this child is the greatest in the kingdom of heaven. And whoever welcomes one such child in my name welcomes me."

Beautiful, right? But what I've never seen in that kids' wing is a second picture right next to the first one, depicting a bloated, drowned body at the bottom of an ocean with a millstone tied around his neck. That would be from the next verses in the "little children" passage (Matthew 18:6–9 NIV), which say:

> If anyone causes one of these little ones—those who believe in me—to stumble, it would be better for them to have a large millstone hung around their neck and to be drowned in the depths of the sea. Woe to the world because of the things that cause people to stumble! Such things must come, but woe to the person through whom they come! If your hand or your foot causes you to stumble, cut it off and throw it away. It is better for you to enter life maimed or crippled than to have two hands or two feet and be thrown into eternal fire. And if your eye causes you to stumble, gouge it out and throw it away. It is better for you to enter life with one eye than to have two eyes and be thrown into the fire of hell.

Graphic stuff! I think this illustration was meant to make us shudder. Jesus is making sure that we're listening. *Do not harm my children.* He makes a strong case for ripping away things from our lives that cause us to stumble in our walk with God. When it comes to our children, should we do any less to protect them?

Saint Paul gave us the positive side of the coin:

Finally, brothers and sisters, whatever is true, whatever is noble, whatever is right, whatever is pure, whatever is lovely, whatever is admirable—if anything is excellent or praiseworthy—think about such things. (Philippians 4:8 NIV)

Does our tech give those things to our kids? Sometimes. Our kids use smartphones and social media for connection, entertainment, and exploration. *And* with those positives come experiences I've shared in the preceding pages, including sharp increases in anxiety, suicidal ideation, self-harm,[12] pornography that normalizes violence and aggressive behavior toward women,[13] and too many stories of child-on-child abuse.[14]

This means that we parents must ask ourselves critical questions:

- Will social media or a smartphone cause my child to stumble?
- Will social media or a smartphone show my child content that's too much, too soon?
- Will social media or a smartphone show my child a steady stream of images and videos that are the opposite of noble, right, pure, lovely, admirable, excellent, or praiseworthy?
- Will social media or a smartphone prevent my child from hearing the whispers of the Holy Spirit?
- Will social media or a smartphone degrade my child's relationship with God?

Then we must ask ourselves: "Is a yes to any of these an example of causing our children to stumble?" Additionally, if the church is doing nothing, isn't its silence also causing children to stumble? What if Jesus is talking about *us*?

Jonathan Haidt, author of *The Anxious Generation*, says this: "From a spiritual perspective, social media is a disease of the mind."[15]

That's a gut punch, but don't we feel it to be true? It's no wonder we walk away from a long scroll session feeling dimmer, drained, and a little more distant.[16] Even as an adult with a (somewhat) steadier brain and thicker emotional skin, I can't remember a time I left Instagram saying, "Wow, I feel like I'm flourishing!" If that's how social media leaves me, what must it be doing to our kids? And why aren't faith leaders everywhere raising the alarm—urging families to take the intentional, life-giving road of #delayistheway? Once again, it takes superhero parents to take back control of childhood innocence. We need to demand more from those who tend the flock in our churches. Talk to your youth and children's pastors, your senior pastor, or any councils in your church and raise this issue. What is your church doing to protect the spiritual life of kids in the digital age? What is the phone policy in youth group? What protections are in place, even on church Wi-Fi? Are pictures of kids posted on the church's public social media accounts (remember, deepfakes happen)? Is the use of AI glamorized by youth pastors and volunteers? The church cannot be silent on the spiritual disease coming for our children—we've got to talk about it.

The World We Want to Live In

Now that you're an expert on our Five Habits framework, which gives structure to your digital parenting in your home, some of you also have what it takes to activate your digital parenting superpowers outside of the home.

I recently had a cordial disagreement with a political libertarian on a post. He told me very plainly, "Chris, I don't believe in collective (societal) responsibility toward children."

This was my response:

I wish we lived in a world where we could rely on our citizens to steward personal liberty responsibly and do no harm to my kids. But we don't live in that world.

I wish we lived in a world where laissez-faire economics also meant that companies cared about keeping my children safe online. But we don't live in that world.

Childhood has always had risks. But back then, an analog childhood plus strict, intentional parents often meant that you mostly stayed away from egregious harm.

Sure, we still snuck a drink. Sure, we still saw a few magazines or a VHS tape. But these activities required intense planning, effort, and a flowchart to pull off if you had intentional parents.

There is a big difference today. Now the egregious harm is in our kids' pockets. The egregious harm is on the same thing where you learn language arts. The egregious harm is on what Dad uses for work with a VPN.

In my experience—both as a father and after thousands of conversations with parents globally—*no amount of careful, intentional parenting in the digital age brings the risk of egregious harm down to an acceptable level without help from other layers in society.*

I desperately want a world where all societal layers—parents, companies, schools, and governments—adequately steward their duty of care toward children. And I 10,000 percent agree that millions of parents need to *grow a backbone and just say "no."*

But, in my opinion, even when parents do their part, if companies and schools are not performing their jobs, the amount and intensity of harm that can still be wrought on my child is unacceptable. Like the post-Enron era I lived through as a business leader . . . which created a framework, liability, and penalties, I'd like to see a child-safe design framework adopted, a few surgical policies passed,[17] personal liability for executives, and significant penalties for companies who ignore these new rules.

I hope for a time when these things are true—a time when all layers in society are helping to create safer digital spaces.

I'm not asking society to do the job of parents. I'm simply asking that companies stop making things more difficult and provide common sense protections—or pay through the nose. If we all ask—if we all *demand*—change, progress might begin. In fact, parents around the world are reclaiming childhood.[18]

Everyone can do something—even you!

- Identify an issue from the priorities just given that matters to you. It could be a law about pornography, a no-phone policy in schools, or better device rules on church mission trips. Talk to the youth pastor at your church, share the research about brains and tech, and ask them to create policies allowing for the still, quiet voice of the Holy Spirit on church-sponsored events. Resources for motivated parents are more abundant than ever.[19]
- Find out who represents you in government and send them an email (they all have "contact me" forms on their website). If you can, request a meeting with their staff. Share what matters to you! Again, most citizens aren't aware of the access we have to our elected officials. You can even fly to Washington, DC, visit a congressional office, and meet with staff if you want to. But start small and see where that takes you.
- Find a parent liaison at school or begin attending school board meetings, where you might make a public comment about distraction-free learning or the use of EdTech and AI in the classroom. Leverage existing templates and talking points created by others as a starting point.[20]

Friends, the dangerous swimming pool is now in kids' pockets and it's teeming with sharks. You've taken ownership of protecting and preparing *your* kids online. That's essential. But now maybe it's time to own what you can control and expand your influence. More action is desperately needed—for your kids and for mine.

All Things Are Possible

Admittedly, what I've asked of you in the Five Habits is daunting:

- Be an expert in self-evaluation (Habit 1).
- Practice anger management (Habit 2).
- Understand child development (Habit 3).
- Have a basic grasp of brain science (Habit 4).
- Apply parental controls (Habit 5).

At the same time, many of you are also considering how to keep your child pointed toward Jesus. Piece of cake, right?

If I had offered you that formidable list in the introduction, you might have quit.

But you didn't! You *can* do these things! Now that you've armed yourself with explanations, stories of hope, connection to science and Scripture, and possible solutions, don't you feel that it's possible? That by doing certain *small* things consistently and persistently, you might just have a fighting chance against this problem.

I believe you can do this—by controlling what you can control.

Power to the Parents

Dr. Mitch Prinstein, the former chief of psychology for the American Psychological Association, once told me, "Chris, there are no findings showing harm to children who stay off social media. In fact, some emerging evidence suggests that the most socially competent kids are refraining from using these platforms."

Deep down, you know Dr. Prinstein's words are true, don't you?

The messages I receive from Protect Young Eyes followers have a similar tone. I see a bunch of powerful, awesome parents who are:

- **Defiant.** Your child gets one, precious childhood. Big Tech can't have it.
- **Strong.** You don't win every battle—but you keep trying to do what's best.
- **Brave.** You're willing to walk alone *if you must.*

But now, with maybe millions more in agreement,[21] you don't need to feel overwhelmed. When we give our children a chance to be kids and young people with limited digital interference, something amazing happens. We raise tech-wise, morally grounded, and resilient kids in a connected world.

Drip by drip, step by step, and chat by chat, you are a strong digital parent—proactive, discerning, and values-conscious—building a smart, tech-ready family. You've joined a movement of families who protect without panic, train without fear, and guide with grace and grit. Today, with one little conversation, show your family how to look up in awe, reach out with care, and experience wonder. Our kids were created to perform these beautiful activities. And nothing in the digital world can do a better job of showing your kids how to do them than *you.*

5 Takeaways for Parents

1. **Protecting kids online is a shared effort:** Even careful parents can't shield children from all digital dangers—society, schools, and tech companies must help.
2. **Treat smartphones like "digital swimming pools":** Just as pools require gates for safety, tech needs built-in protections like age verification and child-safe designs.

3. **Advocate for better laws and accountability:** Parents can push for policies that protect kids online, such as requiring age checks and limiting harmful content.
4. **Faith communities should speak up:** The church and other moral voices must address the spiritual and emotional risks of digital life for children.
5. **Parents have real power:** By setting limits, educating others, and working together, families can reclaim childhood from Big Tech and nurture healthier, grounded kids.

"Do Just Two Things This Week" Checklist

☐ Learn about your state's approach to phones in schools here: https://www.anxiousgeneration.com/policy-state-map. Learn about your state's approach to age-verifying pornography sites here: https://www.exoduscry.com/pcnp/tracker/.

☐ Identify your state representatives and senators. Consider signing up for their newsletters.

How to Talk About Porn with Your Kid

In the Habit 2 chapter, we talked about facing our fears and making talking about porn the norm with your kids. Now that we are armed with a more complete understanding of why our kids are vulnerable to porn and its impacts, let's go through practical scenarios and illustrative talking points to help you be calm and confident, no matter how old your kids may be. Let's start on the early side.

How to Talk to a Young Child About Porn

We're always looking for opportunities to build authentic connection with our kids, especially when it comes to tough conversations. This means I want their curiosities to end with us. I want to rob the devil of his curiosity power over our children regarding certain stimulating topics like pornography.

One time, a father named Anthony approached me after a parent presentation at a local charter school. "Chris, my five-year-old likes to use our tablet," he began. "What should I say to him so that he uses it well? Do I talk about pornography? What should I do?"

These are great questions!

When parents ask, "What's the right age to talk to a child about pornography?" here are my standard responses:

- I don't know your family, but if you wait until you're ready, it's too late.
- I don't know your family, but your kids are ready for the talk before you are. Just get it done!
- Does your kid ride a school bus? Then he/she needs to know the word and what to do when (not if) they hear it.

Let's continue the conversation I was having with Anthony about his five-year-old son.

Is a five-year-old ready to hear about pornography? Kind of. Do you need to use the word *pornography* with your kindergartner? No. But should your child still know what to do when they see someone without their clothes on? Absolutely! This means you need to be specific and help them understand the larger concept of pornography and inappropriate content by using age-appropriate language.

I think kids are ready to handle conversations of this nature far sooner than their parents are. Let's keep in mind that the average age of a child's first exposure to explicit online content is somewhere in the tween years, according to almost any study.[1] They need to be ready. So, I told Anthony that at age five he has a fantastic opportunity to lay a foundation of trust and transparency with his boy.

I gave Anthony a very tangible illustration to use the next time he spoke to his son. He might say,

Hey, you know that your dad would do anything to protect you, right? Good. So, just pretend something for a minute. Imagine that you're out in the woods with your friends, walking down a trail, and something really scary happened. An animal or even a person jumped out and scared you. You would tell me about that, right? I know you would.

Well, every time you use this iPad, it's like going for a walk in the woods. The internet gives us all kinds of trails we can walk down when we click around on games and have fun. Now, me or Mom are going to probably be right here with you when you use the iPad, but if you ever see anything weird or scary—or something that shows people without their clothes on—and we're not right there with you, promise me that you'll tell either of us all about it, okay? I'll never, ever be mad if you tell me. Remember, I want to protect you!

For a five-year-old, this type of conversation is a great start. It's tangible, understandable, and foundational. And when paired with "practice, practice, practice" in Habit 2, it's powerful prevention. Granted, Anthony still needs to have follow-up conversations regularly and can continue building up these conversations as his son gets older. I believe that talks like this begin creating a family culture of trust and transparency so that kids know what to do when they see something inappropriate, whether they're five or fifteen.

"PUT IT DOWN AND TELL SOMEONE"

An important age-appropriate foundation for this conversation with little ones is making sure your kids know about their body parts. Here's a little scenario as an example. Imagine a mom standing with her five-year-old son at the kitchen island.

Mom: "Hi! I see you're using the iPad. That's great. You like using it, don't you?"

Son: "Yeah, Mom, I love this thing."

Mom: "Well, put it down for just a second. Cool. [name], you know what your private parts are, right?"

Son: "Um, yep. I sure do." (Come on, now . . . he's a five-year-old boy. If you've raised boys, you know what I'm talking about!)

Mom: "Okay, great. Now, Mom or Dad will usually be with

you when you're using the iPad, but if you ever see anything weird, scary, or uncomfortable—if you ever see someone else's private parts, do you know what I want you to do?" (Now he's really listening.)

Son: "No, what?"

Mom: "I want you to put it down and tell someone. That's it! Can you say that back to me?"

Son: "Sure, put it down! Tell someone!"

Mom: "That's awesome, buddy! Can you give me an example of someone you might tell?"

Son: (thinking) "Aunt Susie, Dad, Grandma, you."

Mom: "Yes! Exactly! Awesome job, [name]. You can always tell me. Okay?"

Whenever this mom remembered to check in, she would ask her son, "Hey, [name], what do you do if you ever see something strange or any private parts on the internet?"

The son would then tell his mom, "I put it down, and tell someone."

Good deal—a mother just taught her five-year-old son what to do when he sees pornography, and she never had to say the actual word. Guess what? Now that her son is six and sometimes rides the school bus, he's ready to learn the word *pornography* and knows what to do if he ever hears it. "Tell someone!" No big deal—it's just a word. Here's what the conversation at age six might look like:

Mom: "[name], do you remember when I told you about seeing weird things on the internet? Like someone's private parts?"

Son: "Sure, Mom."

Mom: "Well, there's a word for that. It's called 'pornography.' And, if you ever hear a kid say the word *pornography*, do you know what I want you to do?"

Son: "What, Mom?"

Mom: "Same as before! Just tell someone. Tell me! No big deal—sound good?"

Son: "Yep!"

Now, here's a pro tip: If you use these tactics and you establish a list of "someones" that your child can tell, be sure all these people know they're on the list! It's important to avoid a situation where your child does the right thing but is made to believe they did the wrong thing, creating confusion and doubt. For example, let's say my son knows to "put it down and tell someone," and he's watching a show on Grandma's smart TV. If he sees something inappropriate and says, "Grandma, there's private parts on the smart TV!" and Grandma freaks out, that's a big deal. Here's why.

My son loves Grandma, and he wouldn't want to do something to make Grandma upset. So, if my son does what Dad said and tells Grandma, but this causes Grandma to sound upset, my son's mind is full of very confusing dialogue. That is where shame can settle in—and he may not say anything the next time something happens. So, to protect that connection with your child, make sure your "someones" are prepared.

How to Talk to Tweens and Teens About Porn

"But, Chris, my daughter is nine! And we haven't started! Am I a failure?" *No.* But I also don't want you to strap your child to a chair in the kitchen and say "pornography" five times to check a box. I don't want you to drown them with a porn talk. Instead, address this subject in smaller doses—drip by drip—throughout their lives. When we give continuous guidance on this topic, they see us as the authority. You don't need to read them a research paper, and they don't need to clap when you're finished. Just talk!

During the tween and early teen years, you'd be surprised at what qualifies for a porn talk. For instance, you could try a time when your kids are receptive, like car time, mealtime, together time, or bedtime.

Say you're driving down the road and your child is a captive audience: "Honey, if you ever see anything that makes you uncomfortable, like naked people on a screen, that's called pornography, and you can tell me. I'm safe!" That's obviously a porn talk. Or you could be in the kitchen making food—and your kids don't even have to be looking at you! You could say, "Guys, have you ever seen anything that makes you uncomfortable? You know that little funny feeling in your belly? Just know that if you ever see this type of thing, you'll never freak me out and you'll never be in trouble by telling me." That's a porn talk. Maybe you're tucking your child in at night and could just say, "Honey, have you ever seen anything uncomfortable, like something that bothers you on a screen, a Chromebook, or a tablet, even while doing homework?" Then listen to their response. That's a porn talk!

Related to our teens, it's almost impossible to be too direct. We use the word itself and explain porn's ugly realities. Visit Fight the New Drug's website (https://www. fightthenewdrug.org) and read *It's Time to Talk to Your Kids About Porn* by Greta Eskridge for help.

The kitchen idea I just mentioned came from a mom who approached me after a presentation and told me that she was trying to have more frequent conversations with her tween and teen kids about tough tech issues. One time, she was stirring soup in the kitchen and blurted out, "Hey, you can always tell me if you see anything inappropriate on a screen, okay?" She didn't know then who did or didn't hear her. Fast-forward two weeks. The mom was tucking her twelve-year-old daughter in for the night, and before she closed the door, her daughter said, "Mom, you said I can tell you anything, right?" She then proceeded to share something she saw on an iPad that bothered her.

Friends, that's a porn talk. Let me remind you of Deuteronomy 6:5–9, where God told the Hebrews to essentially be a divine algorithm in the lives of their children. Let's talk to our kids about everything.

Remember, if they're not just a little annoyed that you're going to that subject again, then you're not doing it enough!

(For Parents) How to Help a Teen Looking at Porn

Pornography is everywhere.

But how will you respond? The focus of this section is to give you steps you might follow if you discover your child is watching porn. There isn't an exact prescription, and although we've numbered these steps 1–2–3, etc., they're not meant to be a rigid sequence.

1. **Don't freak out. Don't freak out. Don't freak out.** Wait for the right opportunity when you're not in panic mode. You won't get another chance to have the first talk, and too many parents try to talk when emotions are high. Don't do it!
2. Be intentional about who is involved in the conversation. For example, if a daughter is using porn, she might be embarrassed to have her father join the initial conversation. The same is true in the opposite situation between a son and a mom. You know the relationship dynamics best—just remember that there's likely going to be a lot of shame attached to this behavior, so use your judgment.
3. Remind your son/daughter that nothing they *do* will ever change the way you *feel*. You still love them deeply.
4. Calmly present the digital evidence that you found.
5. Share reasons why pornography hurts people. Fight the New Drug does an amazing job of explaining why porn is bad for the brain, the heart, and the world.
6. Close the digital doors that allow inappropriate access. Please visit our device and app guides for software suggestions.
7. Allow an opportunity to confess in prayer. If Catholic, have them confess sacramentally.

8. Maybe work together to find a passage of Scripture that will encourage and strengthen you and your child. Memorize it!

9. Place an appropriate punishment, calmly, as you see fit. Loving consequences are fine and necessary. This should include removing whatever device is causing the issue.

Start this discussion with calm and end with consequences, but never do the opposite. If you drop the hammer first, your child will never hear "everything will be okay."

5 Signs Your Child Might Need Professional Help

Parents sometimes ask us how to know if their child needs extra help. This list of behaviors that require outside intervention was compiled from various conversations I've had with counselors over the years:[2]

- Your child's behavior is excessive.
- Your child can't seem to stop viewing pornography, even after intervention.
- Your child's pornography preferences are hardcore, bizarre, and/or illegal.
- Your child has attempted to engage in sexual activity with strangers met online.
- Your child says they want to see a counselor.

Please note: This list is not a medical diagnosis—we aren't licensed counselors. The point is, don't be shy about asking for help.

For additional help talking to your kids about pornography, see appendix 3, "Recommended Tech Resources."

Is It Too Late to Delay? What If My Kids Already Have Tech?

Maybe you read chapter 5 and thought, *Uh-oh—it's too late to delay for us. My kids already have access to gaming and social media.* Don't worry! We have help for parents who find themselves on either side of the spectrum regarding kids and tech:

1. My kid already has it and I'm **not** taking it away. What can I do to keep them safe?
2. My kid already has it, and I **must** take it away. How do I do that?

Camp 1: "I'm Not Taking the Tech Away"

If you're in the first category, maybe you've already provided some tech—maybe too soon—but you don't want to take it away. Still, saying yes too soon increased digital risk for your child. It's time to mitigate that risk, and I believe the best way to do that is to **get ridiculous**:

- ridiculously frequent talks
- ridiculously involved monitoring

- ridiculously direct words
- ridiculously observant parents
- ridiculously engaged connections
- ridiculously informed research
- ridiculously focused on IRL (in real life) interactions

Take the information you've learned in this book and really run with it, for however long it takes to make your kids start to expect the ridiculousness. For support, join our digital coaching community, The Table, and stay up-to-date with ever-changing information and tips by receiving our Download newsletter and following other organizations doing similar work. Make yourself your kids' indispensable tech ally.

Camp 2: "We Need Some Changes. I'm Taking Tech Away."

Are you just done with all tech? Be prepared for a reaction from your kids' developing brains.

A child therapist shared this illustration on the Gabb Wireless blog:[1]

If a vending machine at your high school suddenly stopped dispensing your favorite treat, would you just shrug and walk away? I wouldn't.

I would try again, and if that didn't work, I would pound on the glass, reach up the drop box (which never works), and let a few choice words escape my mouth. . . .

Once I finally realized that my angry outburst won't change the vending machine's behavior, I would stop pushing. I may come back a while later and check again to be sure, but largely I will accept it doesn't work anymore and calm down.

Some young brains simply can't manage today's addictive digital spaces. After a recent presentation, a grandma, who is the guardian for her eleven-year-old grandson, approached me about his addiction to his VR goggles. She was joined by two good friends, who were clearly with her as a sign of support (like-minded tribe for the win!). They seemed to know what was going on and were equally concerned. She shared that he played VR games for hours a day. When she tried to take them away, he wasn't violent toward her but verbally went into fits of rage and would storm out of the house, going away on his bike for hours.

Here's the deal: for some kids—whether it's video games, VR goggles, or social media—it's going to be hard. So, pray and get ready for resistance. Remember, they're not primarily mad at you. *Their brain is mad* at the loss of quick dopamine. Their limbic system is ticked and is not getting a good response to the question "Am I loved?" But since you know from what you've learned that this is going on, you're equipped to respond with grace and truth (John 1:14).

Here are twelve steps to take toward freeing your child from addictive tech:

1. **Pray about the decision.** Invite the Holy Spirit in to create openings, calm, and receptivity.
2. **Be a united front.** For two-parent families, or for kids with multiple homes or guardians, make a clear decision as a unit and commit to this. You first must be on the same page and decide together that the tech is harmful and needs to be removed.
3. **Be loving but firm.** Say no clearly and calmly. Expect pushback but stay consistent. Don't justify endlessly.
4. **Adopt a humble mindset.** Remember, this is on us as parents, not on our kids. Their response is at least partially due to a mistake we made. We can own this lapse in front of them. Try words like:

- "This decision isn't about punishment; it's about your well-being."
- "You won't love much of this—and I'll listen to what you say about it."
- "I allowed you to access something that's not helping you thrive. That's my fault—not yours."
- "Here's what I've observed . . ."
- "Here are the impacts I'm concerned about . . ."

5. **Explain the "why."** Continue step 4 by explaining the *why* in age-appropriate terms: Social media and video games can affect mental health, sleep, self-esteem, and focus. Use words from what you've read earlier in this book. Also use real-world examples or documentaries (e.g., *The Social Dilemma, Childhood 2.0, Can't Look Away: The Case Against Social Media*—always preview these before showing them to your children).

6. **Create a transition plan with their input.** Cold turkey is best for younger children or when usage is low. Gradual withdrawal is for teens who are more heavily dependent; reduce time/features over one to two weeks. Allow them to wrap up their existing chats or conversations and give them a chance to let their friends know what's happening.

7. **Remove access and accounts.** Delete apps from all devices and disable or delete accounts. (Don't just log out.) Use parental controls to block reinstallation.

   Social media accounts like Instagram,[2] Snapchat,[3] X (Twitter),[4] TikTok,[5] and Facebook[6] can all be deactivated or deleted. Some have a thirty-day "reinstatement" period that can be used from a desktop PC. If you think this is something your child might exploit, call this out to let them know that you know and they aren't to do this.

8. **Offer alternatives and seek their input.** Fill the screen void with activities: sports, art, volunteering, music, family outings, and board games. Encourage in-person friendships.

9. **Detox together (model the right behaviors!).** Consider a family-wide digital detox. Remove social media from your own phone too!

10. **Monitor and support emotional withdrawal.** Expect mood swings and boredom. Offer empathy, structure, and alternatives—don't give the phone back just to stop discomfort.

11. **Join a support community.** You can find your tribe in groups like The Table, our PYE private support community,[7] or similar parent communities for support and encouragement.

12. **Stay committed long-term.** Remember: You're protecting your child's brain and well-being. Revisit your goals and stay strong.

After my conversation with the grandma struggling with her grandson's VR addiction, she decided it was time to take the VR goggles away for good. This commitment was met by affirming nods and support from her friends. She knew what she was going to experience—a very angry young man. Thankfully, equipped with knowledge about the "why," caring friends who encouraged her during our conversation, and my blessing, she left feeling strong and confident.

Be encouraged: You can also do this, and your kids *will* see the light at the end of the tunnel. One mom wrote to say: "We actually just removed our TV from our living room. While there has been a bit of a "withdrawal" period for the past few days, it's been great to see the kids spending time outside longer, playing imaginatively with each other, and devoting more of their attention to looking at books or making crafts." They're getting it, and that's a thing of beauty.

Recommended Tech Resources

This information is curated from Protect Young Eyes' recommended items and guides. Use these tools as part of the layered approach we discuss in the Habit 5 chapter: relationships → router → devices → locations → apps.

Family Media Plan Guide

Use this when applying what you learned in Chapter 2 about establishing your family's values and creating a family media plan.

When It's Time to Hand Over a Device

Consider writing your child a letter when they get their first smartphone and/or social media account. Here's an example letter that you can customize:

Kid-Friendly Phones and Wearables

1. BARK PHONE

WHAT IT IS

A kid phone that bakes Bark's monitoring, web blocking, and screen time tools directly into the device,
giving parents granular control over apps, texting, and
browsing.[1] This is the PYE-preferred phone for kids.

WHY IT HELPS

- One ecosystem: Device + monitoring means fewer setup
  pitfalls and fewer "loopholes."
- Strong middle step: Allows talk/text and carefully permitted
  apps before letting kids have a full smartphone. It supports
  our "tech in steps" pathway: watch → limited phone (no
  browser/apps) → add browser/apps when ready.
- **Quick start:** Activate Bark alerts, set app permissions up
  front, and review notifications together with your child
  weekly (builds trust + digital literacy).

2. GABB PHONE

WHAT IT IS

A locked-down starter phone—no open browser; social media either
absent or highly limited depending on plan. Great for talk/text +
GPS.

WHY IT HELPS

- Minimizes exposure while teens mature executive function.
- Familiar "smartphone look" without the rabbit holes that trip
  up beginners.
- **Quick start:** Begin on the most restrictive plan; revisit
  privileges at predefined milestones (e.g., successful school
  quarter, consistent family tech habits).

3. PINWHEEL PHONE

WHAT IT IS

A curated-app ecosystem for kids; internet/social options are intentionally constrained; GPS tracking supported. Available in USA, UK, and Canada (but regularly expanding, so keep checking the PYE Catalog of First Phone Options for updates).

WHY IT HELPS

- Adds flexibility vs. a "no-apps" phone while still filtering the app store to kid-appropriate choices.
- **Quick start:** Start with only essential utility apps (calls, messages, maps). Add apps slowly after "teach → try → review" cycles.

4. GABB WATCH (KID-WEARABLE)

WHAT IT IS

A talk/text GPS watch that keeps kids connected to caregivers without handing them the full internet. Good for younger kids with activities.

WHY IT HELPS

- Contact + location without social feeds; lowers pressure for early phones.
- **Quick start:** Limit contacts to a tight circle; rehearse when/how to use SOS/location features.

5. BARK WATCH (KID-WEARABLE)

WHAT IT IS

Like Gabb, a children's smartwatch with built-in parental protections and no distractions—no games, no browser apps. Intended as a safer "first tech" device with talk/text and GPS. Unique feature includes linkage to Bark's monitoring system—texts, photos, and communications get checked for risks like bullying, inappropriate content, or predatory behavior—and parents get alerts only when something concerning is detected.

- Contact + location without social feeds; lowers pressure for early phones.
- **Quick start:** Limit contacts to a tight circle; rehearse when/how to use SOS/location features.

Home Wi-Fi and Network Layers

GRYPHON ROUTER (AX/GUARDIAN)

WHAT IT IS

A family-centric router line with powerful filtering, device grouping, time limits, and the ability to enforce YouTube Restricted Mode network-wide. I use Gryphon at home and consider it as a top choice after testing multiple routers.

WHY IT HELPS

- "Chokepoint" control: Everything connected to home Wi-Fi inherits guardrails (great for smart TVs and game consoles).
- Better coverage + app-based management reduces the need for piecemeal device setups.
- **Quick start:** Install, create kid/device groups, lock in SafeSearch/Restricted Mode, and schedule default "downtime" windows (dinner, bedtime).

BARK HOME (ATTACH TO EXISTING ROUTERS)

WHAT IT IS

A hardware add-on that connects to your current router to add stronger parental controls (screen time, app blocking) without replacing the router.

- Great for families who like their router but want Bark's controls at the network layer.
- **Quick start:** Pair Bark Home to your router, install the parent app, and begin with broad categories (games, video) before fine-tuning.

Parental Controls and Monitoring

BARK PREMIUM (SOFTWARE)

WHAT IT IS

AI-assisted monitoring that scans texts, email, social media, and device activity for digital dangers; provides alerts, screen time tools, and web blocking. I highly recommend Bark, even though it doesn't see everything on an iPhone—refer to Layer 3 in chapter 6 for the reason!

WHY IT HELPS

- Surfaces *signals* (e.g., cyberbullying, predation cues, self-harm language) without parents reading every message—preserves dignity while protecting.
- **Quick start:** Set alert sensitivity, choose notification channels (email/text), and agree on a family review cadence ("We check alerts together each Sunday").

APPLE SCREEN TIME (IPHONE/IPAD)

WHAT IT IS

Built-in iOS controls for app limits, content restrictions, downtime, and communication safety features. Refer to the PYE device guides for help to correctly configure these constantly changing settings.

WHY IT HELPS

- No extra cost; tight integration; supports "incremental freedoms" with Ask to Buy feature and age-based media limits.
- **Quick start:** Create a child Apple ID in Family Sharing, set Downtime, App Limits, Communication Limits, Communication Safety, and Content & Privacy Restrictions where available.

GOOGLE FAMILY LINK (ANDROID/CHROMEBOOK)

WHAT IT IS

Google's family toolset for supervising Android phones and Chromebooks—location, app approvals, time limits, and filters. Like with Apple, refer to the PYE device guides for help to correctly configure these constantly changing settings.

WHY IT HELPS

- Consistent controls across Android + ChromeOS; essential if your school issues Chromebooks.
- **Quick start:** Add your child to your Family Group, require approvals for new apps, and set school day/bedtime schedules.

COVENANT EYES (ACCOUNTABILITY/FILTERING)

WHAT IT IS

Accountability + filtering with reports to an ally—aimed especially at adults/older teens and families pursuing open, honest tech use. Covenant Eyes is what I used along with allies to break free from long-time compulsive porn use.

WHY IT HELPS

- Moves the conversation from secretive to supportive; powerful for families practicing transparency around explicit content.
- **Quick start:** Decide who receives reports, set goals together, and pair with a home router filter to reduce temptation "at the source."

Streaming, Video, and Smart Speakers

SMART TVS

Since smart TVs have similar access logistics as smartphones, setup and control of the related apps on a smart TV are just as important as steps we might take on an iPhone. This starts with Layer 2, our router,  includes Layer 3 by ensuring that the device (the smart TV itself) is set up correctly, and applies Layer 5 by ensuring that the apps on the smart TV have separate profiles for kids and adults.

    Location: https://www.protectyoungeyes.com/devices/

YOUTUBE/YOUTUBE KIDS

Our "Ultimate Guides" to YouTube and YouTube Kids explain why setup is complex and show how to lock in safer defaults (Restricted Mode, supervised accounts, TV and console scenarios).

    Location: https://www.protectyoungeyes.com/apps/

WHAT TO KNOW

- YouTube appears *everywhere* (phones, TVs, consoles). Router-level enforcement of Restricted Mode plus supervised Google accounts dramatically improves outcomes but isn't foolproof.
- The videos in YouTube Kids aren't always appropriate for kids.[2]
- **Quick start:** Use a supervised Google account for kids, enable Restricted Mode, and reinforce at the router (Gryphon can lock it network-wide). On smart TVs or consoles, make sure the same account settings follow the device.

OTHER STREAMING VIDEO CONSIDERATIONS

A "regular" flatscreen TV can have Wi-Fi streaming access through the following devices:

- Apple TV

- Roku
- Chromecast
- Amazon (Fire TV, Prime Video, Fire Tablets, Fire TV Sticks)

Each has its own set of controls, which you can learn more about at: https://www.protectyoungeyes.com/devices/.

SMART SPEAKER CONSIDERATIONS

Devices like Echo and Google Nest can play music, answer questions, and control smart home gear. They are highly intelligent and often contain explicit-content filters and household rules that can prevent surprises.

Location: https://protectyoungeyes.com/devices/

School and Community Context

Since 44 percent of kids who regularly view pornography have done so on a school-issued device,[3] the Chromebooks and iPads used in education also warrant our "device level" attention. If your school says it's  monitoring everything, be a curious investigator. After all, your school might not have the same digital values you do. You might consider these six questions for school leadership:

1. What are the school's technology policies? Can I inspect them?
2. How much screen time will my child have during the school day, and what digital tools will they be using (hardware and software)?
3. Who at the school evaluates the apps, websites, and AI tools used in classrooms for adherence to privacy and protection standards?
4. Do teachers attend professional development to keep current

on digital trends impacting kids? Do they also learn how to properly and effectively implement digital tools like AI?

5. What network-level filtering and controls exist to protect my child while they are using the school-owned devices, and who is monitoring the network for incidents?

6. What are the alternatives available to those who decide that their child should not use certain digital tools?[4]

Starting this conversation with the school could lead to peace of mind for you and provide a safer digital learning environment for your child.

Parenting Books

- **Dr. Jonathan Haidt, *The Anxious Generation*—**Explores how smartphones and social media contribute to the mental health crisis.

- **Greta Eskridge, *It's Time to Talk to Your Kids About Porn*—**A practical guide for difficult but necessary conversations.

- **Kristen A. Jenson, *Good Pictures Bad Pictures: Porn-Proofing Today's Young Kids*—**A story for ages 8–12 explaining what pornography is, why it's dangerous, and how to reject it.

- **Erin Loechner, *The Opt-Out Family*—**Encouragement for building intentional, less tech-saturated family rhythms.

- **Dr. Michael Reichert, *How to Raise a Boy*—**On building connection and resilience, especially for sons in a digital age.

- **Anything by Dr. Lisa Damour—**Her writing about girls, pressure, and adolescence are essential reading.

- **Anything by Dr. Meg Meeker—**Her writing about dads and daughters significantly influenced my early thinking about being a strong, active father when my daughter was born.

- **Abigail Shrier, *Bad Therapy*—**A critical look at how certain cultural messages intersect with youth struggles.

Experts on AI Trends

AI is changing everything. We do our best to stay current, but a few organizations stay right on the tip of the spear:

- **The Center for Humane Technology—**Listen closely to Tristan Harris, especially his 2025 Ted Talk, "Why AI Is Our Ultimate Test and Greatest Invitation."[5]
- **Project Liberty—**Its weekly newsletter is what I use to stay current on AI developments, and it's good at ending the letter with hope and action.
- **The Brookings Institution—**Particularly its thoughts about AI in schools through the Center for Universal Education.

Acknowledgments

Holy Spirit, you grabbed my heart in college, and in a moment I was transformed. God, I give you praise for this one precious life.

Thank you to former FBI agent and friend Blair for including me in his investigation over a decade ago. I was standing in a hotel hallway in January 2015 when I received a call from WOOD-TV 8 investigative reporter Susan Samples about predators on the Kik app. "Your friend from the FBI said you know what parents can do to protect their kids online," she said. Blair and Susan, I'm grateful for the early trust you had in me to share my untested thoughts with parents.

"Just call it what you want it to do!" was the sage advice I received from Jim Barry, a digital marketing expert, over hot cocoa one winter morning. "It sounds like you want to protect young eyes from this junk," he added. Thank you, Jim—it worked.

"You need a website." Thank you, Rob Kittredge, for offering your time and talents to get something off the ground.

A long list of friends and advocates dot my journey with their friendship, courage, and grit. Doug & Rose Crawford and Michele Lothschutz, you joined me early at PYE and have been my consistent, personal encouragement. Melissa McKay, you've sacrificed your health and endless hours honing the most effective way to rein in tech Goliaths.

Thank you to amazing brothers and sisters on my path: Ben Bull; Dr. Eleanor Kennelly Gaetan; Dawn Hawkins; Peter Gentala; Nicki Petrossi; Sarah Gardner; Lennon Torres; Dr. Mitch Prinstein; Dr. Stacy Drury; Dr.

Jim Winston; Dr. Phil McRae; The Highgate Team; The Human Change Movement; Smartphone Free Childhood; Joe Ryrie; Margarita Louis-Dreyfus; Gaia Berstein; Greta Eskridge; Ashanti Bryant; Tommy McNeil; John DeMay; Lori Schott; Alicia Contro; Ana Villafañe; Pato Giovas; Smith Alley; Collin Kartchner (RIP); Mervyn Arnold; Senator Mike Lee; Blair Bjellos; Colin Anderson; Jan Edwards; Nicole & AJ Morris; Sam Black; Cindy Bultema; Shane Denham; John Parkinson; Scott McClurg; Tim Estes; Ryan Foley; Tracy Foster; Jason & Lisa Frost; Rep. Carol Glanville; Rhonda Graff; Melissa Griffin; Rep. Brandon Guffey; Emily Harrison; Melanie Hempe; Doug Smith; Corissa Sheets; Stefan Joly; Michael Krause; Rick Lane; Jo Lembo; Matt Maines; Katey McPherson; Christina Mehaffey; Lina Nealon; Erin Walker; Leslie Rogers; Brooke Shannon; Lynn Shaw; Tessa Stuckey; Betsy Thompson; Abby Graves; Isaac Taher; Dan Armstrong; Nate Tiemeyer; Jason Walker; Brooke Romney; Titania Jordan; and Andra Zommers. I've forgotten so many, but their DNA is sprinkled throughout these pages.

Dr. Jean Twenge, you risked your reputation to call out the smartphone problem, suffering public persecution and pressure. Thank you for your bravery. Dr. Jonathan Haidt, you kept going after *Coddling of the American Mind* when you could have rested. We are all benefiting from your relentless effort.

To the entire Zondervan and HarperCollins Christian Publishing team, I appreciate your care and professionalism. Deep thanks to Jenn McNeil and Webb Younce for shaping my rough ideas. I learned so much from your patient advice about the art of writing. And how did I ever end up with a running buddy, neighbor, and brother in Christ who just happens to be the world's best literary agent? Thank you, Tom Dean, of A Drop of Ink Literary, for showing me that publishing a book is possible (just like running a two-hundred-mile relay, right?!).

I'm indebted to the countless families who have shared their digital joys and pains with me. I often received a desperate email or direct message on the heels of your tragedy. Many of you simply didn't know you were the subjects of an exploitative experiment. But now we know.

And I pray God will turn your difficult experiences into strength for those who read these chapters.

Finally, Andrea, tonight we were just talking about your rather private role in all of this. Many only know you from the family picture in my talks. But there's **no** PYE without you. You're the one who trusted me to make a midlife career change. I walk through the door after a speaking trip into a home where I'm supported and encouraged. Countless families benefit from *our* partnership in all of this. You're my love.

Notes

Introduction

1. Tim Berners-Lee, "Tim Berners-Lee Announces Creation of the World Wide Web Foundation," speech given to the Knight Foundation, Washington, DC, September 14, 2008, https://webfoundation.org /about/community/transcript-of-tim-berners-lee-video/.

2. Joe Tidy, "Nigerian Brothers Jailed in US for Sextortion Scam Targeting Teenagers," BBC, September 5, 2024, https://www.bbc.com/news /articles/cr7rxpdyz9yo.

3. A statement made by Pastor Jacob Aranza at the Set Free Global Summit, Greensboro, NC, April 6, 2016. A summary of his speech is at https://setfreesummit.org/wednesday/a-biblical-view-of-sexuality -jacob-aranza/.

4. Al Cooper, David Delmonico, Eric Griffinshelley, and Robin Mathy, "Online Sexual Activity: An Examination of Potentially Problematic Behaviors," *Sexual Addiction and Compulsivity* 11, no. 3 (July 2004): 129–43, https://www.researchgate.net/publication/228774926_Online _Sexual_ActivityAn_Examination_of_Potentially_Problematic _Behaviors.

5. According to an informal poll of 2,000 teens by Collin Kartchner, shared with me by the late Collin Kartchner via email.

6. Susan Samples, "Target 8: Download Danger: A Guide for Parents," WoodTV, February 2, 2015, https://www.woodtv.com/news/target-8 -download-danger-a-guide-for-parents/.

7. Quote from Smartphone Free Childhood (UK) (@smartphonefreechildhood) one-year anniversary newsletter, reposted on Protect Young Eyes

(@protectyoungeyes), "Every day we hear stories," Instagram, February 7, 2025, https://www.instagram.com/p/DFy2sQysfdU/.

8. Protect Young Eyes, "Every day we hear stories."

9. Protect Young Eyes, "Every day we hear stories."

10. Anisha Mansuri, "What Is Brainrot and How Do You Know If You Have It?," Healthline, April 22, 2025, https://www.healthline.com/health/what-is-brainrot/.

11. CJ Yatawara, "AI Is Disrupting How Young Brains Grow," Medium, September 4, 2025, https://medium.com/wise-well/ai-is-disrupting-how-young-brains-grow-c1f30196ac63/.

Chapter 1: The Experiment None of Us Signed Up For

1. "Why Should You Study History?" University of Wisconsin–Madison Department of History, accessed December 3, 2025, https://history.wisc.edu/undergraduate-program/why-history/.

2. Jonathan Haidt, *The Anxious Generation: How the Great Rewiring of Childhood Is Causing an Epidemic of Mental Illness* (Penguin, 2024), 9.

3. Michele M. Kroll, "Generation X . . . 'The Forgotten Generation,'" University of New Hampshire Extension, November 1, 2024, https://extension.unh.edu/blog/2024/11/generation-x-forgotten-generation/.

4. Sara Dorn, "'Boy in the Window' in Columbine Massacre Recounts His Escape from Ruthless Killers," *New York Post*, April 6, 2019, https://nypost.com/2019/04/06/boy-in-the-window-in-columbine-massacre-recounts-his-escape-from-ruthless-killers/.

5. These words are preserved on a placard at a memorial in Littleton's Robert F. Clement Park, which contains quotes from those affected by the shooting. See David Pyrooz, "Opinion: The Grim Legacy of Columbine After 25 Years," *Estes Park Trail Gazette*, April 18, 2024, https://www.eptrail.com/2024/04/18/columbine-anniversary-25-years-legacy-shootings/.

6. Paul Farhi, "The 'Crawl' Fed Our Need for Constant News on 9/11. It Never Went Away," *Washington Post*, September 11, 2021, https://www.washingtonpost.com/lifestyle/media/cable-news-crawl-ticker-911/2021/09/10/1219ccc8-0ce5-11ec-a6dd-296ba7fb2dce_story.html/.

7. "American Psyche Reeling from Terror Attacks," Pew Research Center,

September 19, 2001, https://www.pewresearch.org/politics/2001/09/19
/american-psyche-reeling-from-terror-attacks/.

8. "American Psyche Reeling."

9. Claire O'Connor, "Parents' Perceptions of Their Roles and Behaviors
After the 9/11 Terrorist Attack," dissertation, Pace University, 2007,
https://digitalcommons.pace.edu/dissertations/AAI3251232/.

10. Kathy Shalhoub, "My Goal as a Parent Is Not to Make My Kids
Happy—It's to See Them Fulfilled," Motherly, January 13, 2023, https://
www.mother.ly/parenting/my-child-i-want-so-much-more-than
-happiness-for-you/, emphasis original.

11. Consider our posture when using a smartphone or tablet: hunched
over, closed off, and honed in. This is the embodied fulfillment of
the *incurvatus in se* ("curved in on ourselves") attributed to Saint
Augustine and his description of sin. The irony of smartphone use
being the perfect physical illustration for the Augustinian description
of pride (the beginning of all sins) isn't lost on us. See Chris Ritter,
"Speaking of Sin: Augustine, Luther, and the Inward Curve," *The
Gospel Matters* (blog), January 11, 2012, https://thegospelmatters
.wordpress.com/2012/01/11/speaking-of-sin-luther-augustine-and-the
-inward-curv/.

12. Steve Jobs, speech delivered at the Macworld Conference and Expo
2007, San Francisco, January 9, 2007. Transcript at *Singju Post*,
accessed December 4, 2025, https://singjupost.com/wp-content
/uploads/2014/07/Steve-Jobs-iPhone-2007-Presentation-Full
-Transcript.pdf.

13. Doug Bolton, "The Reason Steve Jobs Didn't Let His Children Use
an iPad," *The Independent*, November 1, 2017, https://www.the
-independent.com/tech/steve-jobs-apple-ipad-children-technology
-birthday-a6893216.html/.

14. Mariel Otero del Río, "Why Didn't Steve Jobs Let His Kids Use
iPads?," *Stamford Advocate*, September 18, 2021, https://www
.stamfordadvocate.com/business/article/Why-didn-t-Steve-Jobs-let
-his-kids-use-iPads-16468409.php/.

15. Leah Wankum, "USD 232 School Board Approves Purchase of iPads for
1:1 Elementary Classroom Use," *Johnson County Post*, March 3, 2020,

https://johnsoncountypost.com/2020/03/03/usd-232-school-board
-approves-purchase-of-ipads-for-11-elementary-classroom-use-87510/.

16. Bo Burnham, "Bo Burnham: Colonizing Our Minds in the Age of Social Media," posted November 2, 2022 by Mad Scientist, YouTube, 1:19–2:10, https://www.youtube.com/watch?v=SUTbnjIHfkg&t=144s/.

17. Subcommittee on Crime and Counterterrorism, "A Time for Truth: Oversight of Meta's Foreign Relations and Representations to the United States Congress," U.S. Senate Committee on the Judiciary, April 9, 2025, 1:22:40 to 1:24:27, https://www.judiciary.senate.gov /committee-activity/hearings/a-time-for-truth-oversight-of-metas -foreign-relations-and-representations-to-the-united-states-congress/.

18. Subcommittee on Crime and Counterterrorism, "A Time for Truth," 1:30:14 to 1:30:58.

19. "FBI Violent Crimes Against Children Data," Defend All Kids, accessed January 9, 2026, https://drive.google.com/file/d /1mq2sgKwc8xhPuJrgZ3pfh98I1XfxQ1ag/view?usp=sharing/. The information here is condensed from the full version.

20. Drew Harwell, "A Teen Girl Sexually Exploited on Snapchat Takes On American Tech," *Washington Post*, May 5, 2022, https://www .washingtonpost.com/technology/2022/05/05/snapchat-teens-nudes -lawsuit/.

21. John Doe #1 and John Doe #2 v. Twitter, Inc., First Amended Complaint, Case No. 3:21-cv-00485-JCS (United States District Court, Northern District of California, April 7, 2021), posted at the National Center on Sexual Exploitation, https://endsexualexploitation.org/wp-content /uploads/Doe-v-Twitter_1stAmndComplaint_Filed_040721.pdf.

22. "47 U.S. Code § 230—Protection for Private Blocking and Screening of Offensive Material," Cornell Law School Legal Information Institute, accessed December 4, 2025, https://www.law.cornell.edu/uscode/text /47/230/.

23. NCOSE, "Twitter Lawsuit Reinforces Critical Need to Reform Section 230," National Center on Sexual Exploitation, February 7, 2025, https:// endsexualexploitation.org/articles/twitter-lawsuit-reinforces-critical -need-to-reform-section-230/.

24. Alina Selyukh, "Section 230: A Key Legal Shield for Facebook, Google

Is About to Change," *All Tech Considered* (blog), NPR, March 21, 2018, https://www.npr.org/sections/alltechconsidered/2018/03/21 /591622450/section-230-a-key-legal-shield-for-facebook-google-is -about-to-change/.

25. See John Doe #1 and John Doe #2 v. Twitter, Inc.

26. Ken Dilanian, "Relatives of More Than 60 Young People Who Died of Fentanyl Overdoses File Expanded Lawsuit Against Snapchat," NBC News, April 26, 2023, https://www.nbcnews.com/news/us-news/60 -young-people-died-fentanyl-overdoses-lawsuit-snapchat-rcna81629/.

27. John Tuason, "Roblox: A Tool for Sexual Predators, a Threat for Childrens' Safety," National Center on Sexual Exploitation, July 11, 2024, https://endsexualexploitation.org/articles/roblox-a-tool-for -sexual-predators-a-threat-for-childrens-safety/.

28. "Roblox Platform," RoMonitor Stats, accessed January 5, 2026, https:// romonitorstats.com/platform/.

29. Libby Brooks and Jedidajah Otte, "Risks to Children Playing Roblox 'Deeply Disturbing,' Say Researchers," *The Guardian*, April 14, 2025, https://www.theguardian.com/technology/2025/apr/14/risks-children -roblox-deeply-disturbing-researchers/.

30. Dawn Hawkins, "Prepared Written Testimony," *The World Wild Web: Examining Harms Online*, U.S. House of Representatives Committee on Energy and Commerce, March 26, 2025, https://www.congress.gov/119 /meeting/house/118066/witnesses/HHRG-119-IF17-Wstate-HawkinsD -20250326.pdf.

31. Chris Weller, "Bill Gates and Steve Jobs Raised Their Kids Tech- Free—And It Should've Been a Red Flag," Business Insider, January 10, 2018, https://finance.yahoo.com/news/bill-gates-steve-jobs-shared -182300072.html/.

32. Keith Brannon, "Can Strong Parental Bond Protect Infants Down to Their DNA?," Tulane University, July 21, 2014, https://news.tulane.edu /news/can-strong-parental-bond-protect-infants-down-their-dna/.

33. "Skin-to-Skin Contact," The Baby Friendly Initiative, UNICEF, accessed December 4, 2025, https://www.unicef.org.uk/babyfriendly /baby-friendly-resources/implementing-standards-resources/skin-to -skin-contact/.

34. Catherine Knibbs, *Children, Technology and Healthy Development: How to Help Kids Be Safe and Thrive Online* (Routledge, 2022), 19.

35. Souhir Chamam, Alexia Forcella, Nadia Musio, Florence Quinodoz, and Nevena Dimitrova, "Effects of Digital and Non-Digital Parental Distraction on Parent-Child Interaction and Communication," *Frontiers in Child and Adolescent Psychiatry* 21, no. 3 (2024), https://doi.org/10.3389/frcha.2024.1330331/.

36. Knibbs, *Children, Technology and Healthy Development*, 29.

37. Lisa Damour and Reena Ninan, hosts, *Ask Lisa*, podcast, episode 161, "How Do I Get My Teens to Want to Spend Time with Me?," March 12, 2024, 5:34–5:40, https://drlisadamour.com/resource/how-do-i-get-my-teens-to-want-to-spend-time-with-me/, emphasis mine.

38. Damour and Ninan, "How Do I Get My Teens to Want to Spend Time with Me?," 10:17–11:22.

Chapter 2: Habit 1: Model the Right Behaviors

1. Daniel Sih, *Raising Tech-Healthy Humans: How to Reset Your Children's Tech-Habits and Give Them a Great Start to Life* (Publish Central, 2022), 14–16.

2. "Screen Time for Infants," American Academy of Pediatrics Center of Excellence on Social Media and Youth Mental Health, February 1, 2024, https://www.aap.org/en/patient-care/media-and-children/center-of-excellence-on-social-media-and-youth-mental-health/qa-portal/qa-portal-library/qa-portal-library-questions/screen-time-for-infants/.

3. "The Effects of Screen Time on Children: The Latest Research Parents Should Know," Children's Hospital of Orange County, August 27, 2024, https://health.choc.org/the-effects-of-screen-time-on-children-the-latest-research-parents-should-know/.

4. Brandon T. McDaniel and Jenny S. Radesky, "Technoference: Parent Distraction with Technology and Associations with Child Behavior Problems," *Child Development* 89, no. 1 (2018): 100–109, https://pubmed.ncbi.nlm.nih.gov/28493400/.

5. Chris McKenna with Laurie Krieg, hosts, *Hole in My Heart*, podcast, episode 238, "Screens: From Fighting to Flourishing," March 14, 2025,

https://lauriekrieg.com/podcast/episode-238-screens-from-fighting
-to-flourishing-chris-mckenna/.

6. Theresa H. Rodgers, "Communications Time Bomb: Parents'
Smartphone Use Could Be the New Secondhand Smoke," *USA Today*,
January 16, 2020, https://eu.usatoday.com/story/opinion/2020/01/16
/parents-smartphone-screen-time-new-secondhand-smoke-column
/4448231002/.

7. Rodgers, "Communications Time Bomb."

8. Angela Rozier, "FBI Warns Parents About Increase in Online
Predators," ABC25 WPBF News, August 13, 2025, https://www.wpbf
.com/article/florida-parents-online-predators-school-children
/65743452/.

9. Robert W. Buckingham, "Il Dolce Far Niente: What Simplicity Taught
Me About Life—And Leadership," LinkedIn, September 15, 2025,
https://www.linkedin.com/pulse/il-dolce-far-niente-what-simplicity-
taught-me-life-buckingham-ws9pc/. Emphasis original.

10. Ephrat Livni, "Albert Einstein's Best Ideas Came When He Was
Aimless. Yours Can Too," Quartz, July 20, 2022, https://qz.com
/1299282/albert-einsteins-best-ideas-came-while-he-was-relaxing
-aimlessly-yours-can-too/.

11. Bryan Robinson, "Why Neuroscientists Say, 'Boredom Is Good for Your
Brain's Health,'" *Forbes*, September 2, 2020, https://www.forbes.com
/sites/bryanrobinson/2020/09/02/why-neuroscientists-say-boredom
-is-good-for-your-brains-health/.

12. Jeffrey Kluger, "Why You Get Your Best Ideas in the Shower," *Time*,
July 18, 2024, https://time.com/6999592/shower-thoughts-best-ideas/.

13. Chris McKenna, "I Help Families Create Safer Digital Spaces. Because
Technology Almost Ruined Me," Protect Young Eyes, accessed
December 4, 2025, https://www.protectyoungeyes.com/chris-letter. I
guess I have a thing with sidewalks and epiphanies!

14. Erica Djossa, host, *Momwell*, podcast, episode 184, "Establishing
Family Values: How to Identify What Matters and Avoid Comparison,"
August 2, 2023, https://www.momwell.com/blog/establishing-family
-values/.

15. "Child Sexual Abuse Statistics," National Center for Victims of Crime,

accessed December 4, 2025, https://victimsofcrime.org/child-sexual
-abuse-statistics/.

16. Erin Emmanuel, "Parenting as a Survivor of Childhood Trauma," Trauma
Research Foundation, February 21, 2022, https://traumaresearchfoundation
.org/parenting-as-a-survivor-of-childhood-trauma/.

17. Cindy Robinson, "When Your Childhood Trauma Causes
Overprotective (Digital) Parenting," Protect Young Eyes, March 13,
2023, https://www.protectyoungeyes.com/blog-articles/when-your
-own-childhood-trauma-causes-overprotective-digital-parenting/.

18. Cody Blowers, "#SaveTheKids Packs Snow Canyon High: 'Most
Important App for Your Child Is You,'" *St. George News*, September 14,
2018, https://www.stgeorgeutah.com/news/local/savethekids-packs
-snow-canyon-high-most-important-app-for-your-child-is-you/article
_2dfa35e4-d680-5cdf-9053-93b818ac9b42.html/.

Chapter 3: Habit 2: Pursue Authentic Connection

1. Kristen Senz, "Outrage Spreads Faster on Twitter: Evidence from 44
News Outlets," Harvard Business School, July 13, 2021, https://www
.library.hbs.edu/working-knowledge/hate-spreads-faster-on-twitter
-evidence-from-44-news-outlets/.

2. Meg Meeker, host, *Front Row Dads*, podcast, episode 459, "The
Fatherhood Expert: The Truth about Faith and Child Development,"
October 1, 2024, https://frontrowdads.com/meg-meeker/.

3. Be careful with YouTube Kids. I recommend it only be used by kids
with the "Chosen by You" feature, whereby kids can only watch
the videos that parents have added to an "approved" list. Visit the
app reviews on our website for more information: https://www
.protectyoungeyes.com/apps/.

4. Lisa Damour and Reena Ninan, hosts, *Ask Lisa*, podcast, episode 161,
"How Do I Get My Teens to Want to Spend Time with Me?," March 12,
2024, https://drlisadamour.com/resource/how-do-i-get-my-teens-to
-want-to-spend-time-with-me/.

5. Matthew P. Bergman, "Character.AI Lawsuits," Social Media Victims
Law Center, December 8, 2025, https://socialmediavictims.org
/character-ai-lawsuits/.

6. Learn more about the dangers of AI companions: "AI Companions Are Powerful. Here's Your Complete Guide," Protect Young Eyes, August 13, 2025, https://www.protectyoungeyes.com/blog-articles/complete -guide-to-ai-companions/.

7. "Understanding the Stress Response," Harvard Health Publishing, April 3, 2024, https://www.health.harvard.edu/staying-healthy /understanding-the-stress-response.

8. The phrase "never in trouble" demands some explanation. This doesn't mean there aren't consequences—even John described Jesus as "grace *and* truth" (John 1). The phrase relates more to us parents: "Not in trouble" means no anger from us. This affirms that whatever happened online probably isn't fully our kids' fault and there's nothing they could do to change your unconditional love for them.

9. "Porn Harms the Environment," The Reward Foundation, accessed December 4, 2025, https://rewardfoundation.org/porn-harms-the -environment/.

10. Robert Lopez and Jeff Marx, "The Internet Is for Porn," *Avenue Q: Original Broadway Cast Recording* (RCA Victor, 2003), posted January 19, 2013, by Broadway Classics, YouTube, 3 min., 10 sec., https://www .youtube.com/watch?v=LTJvdGcb7Fs/.

11. "Amount of Content Uploaded to Pornhub Worldwide from 1st Half 2023 to 1st Half 2025, by Format," Statista, accessed December 4, 2025, https://www.statista.com/statistics/1361995/pornhub-pieces-of -content-by-format/.

12. Jordan Valinsky, "Pornhub Removes a Majority of Its Videos After Investigation Reveals Child Abuse," CNN, December 15, 2020, https:// www.cnn.com/2020/12/15/business/pornhub-videos-removed/.

13. Freya India, "What Porn Took from Us," *The Free Press*, June 5, 2025, https://www.thefp.com/p/what-porn-took-from-us/.

14. Lianne Kolirin, "Billie Eilish Says Watching Porn from Age 11 'Really Destroyed My Brain,'" CNN, December 16, 2021, https://edition.cnn .com/2021/12/15/entertainment/billie-eilish-porn-scli-intl/index.html.

15. This is why home routers are so important. If used correctly, all Wi-Fi-dependent devices are filtered all the time. You'll appreciate the power of your router as you learn and apply Habit 5!

16. "If You Struggle with Porn-Induced Erectile Dysfunction, There's Hope for Healing," Fight the New Drug, accessed December 4, 2025, https://fightthenewdrug.org/pied-recovery-hope-for-healing/.

17. Gemma Mestre-Bach, Alejandro Villena-Moya, and Carlos Chiclana-Actis, "Pornography Use and Violence: A Systemic Review of the Last 20 Years," *Trauma, Violence, and Abuse* 25, no. 2 (2024): 1088–1112, https://pubmed.ncbi.nlm.nih.gov/37309642/.

18. Hamida Mubasshera, "Pornography Usage During Adolescence: Does It Lead to Risky Sexual Behavior?," *Journal of Health Economics* 33, no. 8 (2024): 1682–1704, https://pubmed.ncbi.nlm.nih.gov/38511292/.

19. Nancy D. Kellogg, "Sexual Behaviors in Children: Evaluation and Management," *American Family Physician* 82, no. 10 (2010): 1233–38, https://www.aafp.org/pubs/afp/issues/2010/1115/p1233.html/.

20. "10 Before 10. Making Porn a Normal Talk," Protect Young Eyes, May 13, 2024, https://www.protectyoungeyes.com/blog-articles/10-before-10-time-to-make-porn-a-normal-talk/.

21. I love the power of this "do tech together" example—but I don't love Roblox. It's popular with young kids but has a long history of predatory and explicit activity. Please read our full Roblox app review at Protect Young Eyes and do your homework before considering it: https://www.protectyoungeyes.com/apps/roblox-parental-controls/.

22. Andy Stanley, "Fall Worship Series: One Another," Hamline Church, accessed December 4, 2025, https://www.hamlinechurch.org/wordpress/fall-worship-series-one-another/.

23. Chris McKenna, "The Importance of Accountability," Covenant Eyes, October 24, 2024, https://www.covenanteyes.com/blog/can-accountability-change-a-heart/.

24. Robert Nichols, "The Power of Shared Attention: How Infants Learn from Caregivers," Lehigh University, January 29, 2025, https://cas.lehigh.edu/articles/power-shared-attention-how-infants-learn-caregivers/.

25. Brené Brown, host, *Unlocking Us*, podcast, "Esther Perel on New AI—Artificial Intimacy," March 20, 2024, https://brenebrown.com/podcast/new-ai-artificial-intimacy/.

26. John Delony (@johndelony), "When your child starts speaking to

you," Instagram, March 13, 2024, https://www.instagram.com/p/C4eXsmQu5TR/.

27. John Delony (@johndelony), "Make it a regular practice," Instagram, March 24, 2025, https://www.instagram.com/p/DHlmhuTuxDg/.

28. Rick Ansorge, Frances Gatta, and Amy Gopal, "Piaget Stages of Development," WebMD, February 16, 2024, https://www.webmd.com/children/piaget-stages-of-development/.

29. Jill Suttie, "When Do Your Secrets Hurt Your Well-Being?," Greater Good, July 25, 2022, https://greatergood.berkeley.edu/article/item/when_do_your_secrets_hurt_your_wellbeing.

Chapter 4: Habit 3: Encourage Work and Play

1. Rodolfo Llinás, *I of the Vortex: From Neurons to Self* (Bradford, 2002).

2. Ann Kendig, "Sea Squirts and You: Health and Exercise," Mountain Mindset Counseling, November 30, 2017, https://mountainmindsetcounseling.com/2017/11/30/sea-squirts-and-you-health-and-exercise/.

3. "'Brain Rot' Named Oxford Word of the Year 2024," Oxford University Press, December 2, 2024, https://corp.oup.com/news/brain-rot-named-oxford-word-of-the-year-2024/.

4. "Brain Architecture," Harvard University Center on the Developing Child, accessed December 4, 2025, https://developingchild.harvard.edu/key-concept/brain-architecture/.

5. "Our Kids Are the Least Flourishing Generation We Know Of," posted April 1, 2025, by *The Ezra Klein Show*, YouTube, 1 hr., 15 min., 40 sec., https://www.youtube.com/watch?v=RN2GhPal4qA/.

6. Mary Rieck, "Why Young Kids Learn Through Movement [The Atlantic]," Pottstown Trauma Informed Community Connection, May 20, 2016, https://www.pacesconnection.com/g/pottstown-aces-connection/blog/why-young-kids-learn-through-movement-the-atlantic/.

7. Melissa Griffin, "About," HR Mom, accessed December 4, 2025, https://hrmom.com/about/.

8. Liz Mineo, "Good Genes Are Nice, but Joy Is Better," *The Harvard Gazette*, April 11, 2017, https://news.harvard.edu/gazette/story/2017

/04/over-nearly-80-years-harvard-study-has-been-showing-how-to
-live-a-healthy-and-happy-life/.

9. Lan Nguyen, Jared Walters, Siddharth Paul, Shay Monreal Ijurco, Georgia E. Rainey, Nupur Parekh et al., "Feeds, Feelings, and Focus: A Systematic Review and Meta-Analysis Examining the Cognitive and Mental Health Correlates of Short-Form Video Use," *Psychological Bulletin* 151, no. 9 (2025): 1125–46, https://pubmed.ncbi.nlm.nih.gov /41231585/.

10. "Slow vs Fast Dopamine: How to Boost Dopamine Naturally," Unplugged, August 6, 2024, https://unplugged.rest/blog/slow-vs-fast -dopamine/.

11. Mineo, "Good Genes Are Nice."

12. "Slow vs Fast Dopamine."

13. "Executive Function," Cleveland Clinic, March 15, 2024, https://my .clevelandclinic.org/health/articles/executive-function/.

14. Tiffany Nieslanik, "Letting Kids Run Wild Outside Is Surprisingly Good for Their Brains," *National Geographic*, August 20, 2025, https:// www.nationalgeographic.com/health/article/feral-child-summer -outdoor-play-brain-benefits/.

15. Jackie Mader, "Want Resilient and Well-Adjusted Kids? Let Them Play," The Hechinger Report, November 14, 2022, https://hechingerreport.org /want-resilient-and-well-adjusted-kids-let-them-play/.

16. Hillary Wilkinson and Lenore Skenazy, hosts, *Healthy Screen Habits*, podcast, season 9, episode 7, "Let Go and Let Grow for Healthy, Independent Kids!," March 20, 2024, https://www.healthyscreenhabits .org/s9-episode-7-let-go-and-let-grow-for-healthy-independent-kids -lenore-skenazy/.

17. Wilkinson and Skenazy, "Let Go and Let Grow."

18. Jane E. Brody, "Parenting Advice from 'America's Worst Mom,'" *New York Times*, January 19, 2015, https://archive.nytimes.com/well.blogs .nytimes.com/2015/01/19/advice-from-americas-worst-mom/.

19. Katherine Schulten, "How Much Freedom Have Your Parents Given You?," *New York Times*, January 29, 2015, https://archive.nytimes.com /learning.blogs.nytimes.com/2015/01/29/how-much-freedom-have -your-parents-given-you/.

20. Wilkinson and Skenazy, "Let Go and Let Grow."

21. Andrew Sleighter (@andrew_sleighter), "Get out there and break stuff kids!," TikTok, September 16, 2024, https://www.tiktok.com/@andrew _sleighter/video/7415341235520539947/.

22. Jon Haidt and Peter Gray, "Play Deprivation Is a Major Cause of the Teen Mental Health Crisis," After Babel, July 27, 2023, https://www .afterbabel.com/p/the-play-deficit/.

23. "Caring for Your Mental Health," National Institute of Mental Health, December 2024, https://www.nimh.nih.gov/health/topics/caring-for -your-mental-health/.

24. John J. Ratey and Eric Hagerman, *Spark: The Revolutionary New Science of Exercise and the Brain* (Little, Brown, 2013), 91.

25. Louise Morales-Brown, "What to Know About Runner's High," Medical News Today, September 3, 2020, https://www.medicalnewstoday.com /articles/runners-high/.

26. Ratey and Hagerman, *Spark*, 122.

27. First United Nations Congress on the Prevention of Crime and the Treatment of Offenders, "United Nations Standard Minimum Rules for the Treatment of Prisoners," adopted August 30, 1955, posted on Human Rights Watch, accessed December 4, 2025, https://www.hrw .org/legacy/advocacy/prisons/un-smrs.htm.

28. Tracy Foster, "A Not-So-Smartphone," After Babel, May 13, 2025, https://www.afterbabel.com/p/a-not-so-smartphone/.

Chapter 5: Habit 4: Delay Addictive Technologies

1. "Betty White Snickers Ad (2010)," AdAge, accessed December 5, 2025, https://adage.com/video/betty-white-snickers-ad-2010/.

2. "DSM-5 Criteria for Substance Use Disorders," Gateway Foundation, June 15, 2025, https://www.gatewayfoundation.org/blog/dsm-5 -substance-use-disorder/.

3. "Problematic Use of the Internet: Summary and Recommendations," Children and Screens: Institute of Digital Media and Child Development, January 2025, https://www.childrenandscreens.org /learn-explore/research/problematic-use-of-the-internet-summary -and-recommendations/. Emphasis added.

4. I realize the phrase "most games" is highly subjective. Does the game have variable rewards hidden throughout? Does it connect you with others? Is it beautiful and engaging? But any of these features can be addictive to young brains.

5. "Early Careers," TikTok, accessed December 5, 2025, https://lifeattiktok.com/earlycareers/.

6. Matt Richtel, Catherine Pearson, and Michael Levenson, "Surgeon General Warns That Social Media May Harm Children and Adolescents," *New York Times*, May 23, 2023, https://www.nytimes.com/2023/05/23/health/surgeon-general-social-media-mental-health.html/.

7. Marilyn J. Cipolla, "Anatomy and Ultrastructure," in *The Cerebral Circulation* (Morgan & Claypool Life Sciences, 2009), online at the National Library of Medicine, National Center for Biotechnology Information, accessed December 5, 2025, https://www.ncbi.nlm.nih.gov/books/NBK53086/.

8. "Scientists Build Largest Maps to Date of Cells in Human Brain," National Institutes of Health, October 31, 2023, https://www.nih.gov/news-events/nih-research-matters/scientists-build-largest-maps-date-cells-human-brain/.

9. Robert Sapolsky, "3 Brain Systems That Control Your Behavior: Reptilian, Limbic, Neo Cortex," posted June 25, 2017, by Big Think, YouTube, 7 min., 37 sec., https://www.youtube.com/watch?v=hg6XUYWj-pk/.

10. Sapolsky, "3 Brain Systems," 1:19.

11. Marisa Gerber, "Parents Are Blaming Snapchat for Their Teens' Fentanyl Deaths. Will an L.A. Lawsuit Shape the Future of Social Media?," *Los Angeles Times*, March 5, 2025, https://www.latimes.com/business/story/2025-03-05/snap-lawsuit-fentanyl-death-teens/.

12. Officer [David] Gomez (@deputygomez), "Giving your child social media," Facebook, November 2, 2024, https://www.facebook.com/deputygomez/posts/pfbid037d4s3Dj44B16FL6M3uGkLrHbJq N3KNPayGyLXdfkUKmYBwYf3cHPhp5sCXy5UfgWl/.

13. Chris McKenna, "Kids See Too Much Too Soon," Almost Always Analog, May 21, 2024, https://chriswmckenna.substack.com/p/kids-see-too-much-too-soon/.

14. McKenna, "Kids See Too Much Too Soon."

15. "Children, Violence and Vulnerability 2023," Youth Endowment Fund, November 13, 2023, https://youthendowmentfund.org.uk/reports /children-violence-and-vulnerability-2023/.

16. Catherine M. Lee and Karen A. Bax, "Children's Reactions to Parental Separation and Divorce," *Paediatrics and Child Health* 5, no. 4 (2000): 217–18, https://pmc.ncbi.nlm.nih.gov/articles/PMC2817796/.

17. "How Counselors Help Students Cope with Traumatic Events," Wake Forest University, November 14, 2024, https://counseling.online .wfu.edu/blog/how-counselors-help-students-cope-with-traumatic -events/.

18. "Effects," The National Child Traumatic Stress Network, accessed December 5, 2025, https://www.nctsn.org/what-is-child-trauma /trauma-types/complex-trauma/effects/.

19. McKenna, "Kids See Too Much Too Soon."

20. Jessica S. Flannery, Kaitlyn Burnell, She-Joo Kwon, Nathan A. Jorgensen, Mitchell J. Prinstein, Kristen A. Lindquist et al., "Developmental Changes in Brain Function Linked with Addiction-Like Social Media Use Two Years Later," *Social Cognitive and Affective Neuroscience* 19, no. 1 (2024), https://academic.oup.com/scan/article /19/1/nsae008/7604373?login=false/.

21. Snapchat Support, "How Do Streaks Work and When Do They Expire?," Snapchat, accessed December 5, 2025, https://help.snapchat .com/hc/en-us/articles/7012394193684-How-do-Streaks-work-and -when-do-they-expire/.

22. Snapchat Support, "How Much Does It Cost to Restore a Streak?," Snapchat, accessed December 5, 2025, https://help.snapchat.com/hc /en-us/articles/13086861638676-How-much-does-it-cost-to-restore-a -Streak/.

23. Jon Haidt, "Social Media Is a Major Cause of the Mental Illness Epidemic in Teen Girls. Here's the Evidence," After Babel, February 22, 2023, https://www.afterbabel.com/p/social-media-mental-illness -epidemic/.

24. Subcommittee on Crime and Counterterrorism, "A Time for Truth: Oversight of Meta's Foreign Relations and Representations to the

United States Congress," U.S. Senate Committee on the Judiciary, April 9, 2025, https://www.judiciary.senate.gov/committee-activity /hearings/a-time-for-truth-oversight-of-metas-foreign-relations-and -representations-to-the-united-states-congress/.

25. Haidt, "Social Media Is a Major Cause of the Mental Illness Epidemic in Teen Girls."

26. Protect Young Eyes (@protectyoungeyes), "It's spreading! Are you with me?," Instagram, September 14, 2021, https://www.instagram.com/p /CT0PrGflb6g/.

27. Sam Liberty, "Why Your Child Can't Stop Using That App (A Game Designer's Warning)," Medium, March 31, 2025, https://medium.com /design-bootcamp/why-your-child-cant-stop-using-that-app-a-game -designer-s-warning-f5116c06e0b9/.

28. "Video Gaming May Be Associated with Better Cognitive Performance in Children," National Institutes of Health, October 24, 2022, https:// www.nih.gov/news-events/news-releases/video-gaming-may-be -associated-better-cognitive-performance-children/.

29. "Effects of Video Games on Teen Mental Health," Bright Path Behavioral Health, August 23, 2023, https://www.brightpathbh.com /effects-of-video-games-on-teen-mental-health/.

30. Andrew Fishman, "Video Games Are Social Spaces," *Psychology Today*, August 10, 2025, https://www.psychologytoday.com/us/blog/video -game-health/201901/video-games-are-social-spaces/.

31. "The Lure of the Screen: How Video Games Can Lead to Social Isolation," BlueFire Pulsar, accessed December 5, 2025, https:// bluefirepulsar.com/video-games-social-isolation/.

32. "Violent Video Games Found Not to Be Associated with Adolescent Aggression," University of Oxford, February 13, 2019, https://www.ox .ac.uk/news/2019-02-13-violent-video-games-found-not-be-associated -adolescent-aggression/.

33. Anna T. Prescott, James D. Sargent, and Jay G. Hull, "Metaanalysis of the Relationship Between Violent Video Game Play and Physical Aggression over Time," *Proceedings of the National Academy of Sciences of the United States of America* 115, no. 40 (2018): 9882–88, https://www .pnas.org/doi/10.1073/pnas.1611617114/.

34. See Nicholas Kardaras, "Glow Kids Tech Addiction Research: The Clinical, Neurological and Behavioral Effects of Screens," Dr. Kardaras, accessed January 6, 2026, https://www.drkardaras.com/research .html, and Richard Freed, "The Tragic Story of Child Video Game Addiction," Richard Freed, August 11, 2016, https://www.richardfreed .com/blog/the-compelling-story-of-child-video-game-addiction/.

35. See Jonathan Haidt (@jonathanhaidt), "Healthy (slow) vs. unhealthy (quick) dopamine," Instagram, April 3, 2025, https://www.instagram .com/reel/DH_-VAyOWej/, and Lisa Damour and Reena Ninan, hosts, *Ask Lisa*, podcast, episode 214, "Should I Let My Son Spend All His Free Time Playing Video Games?," April 8, 2025, https://drlisadamour.com /resource/should-i-let-my-son-spend-all-his-free-time-playing-video -games/.

36. "Roblox: Inflated Key Metrics for Wall Street and a Pedophile Hellscape for Kids," Hindenburg Research, October 8, 2024, https:// hindenburgresearch.com/roblox/.

37. Isabel Hogben, "I Had a Helicopter Mom. I Found Pornhub Anyway," *The Free Press*, August 29, 2023, https://www.thefp.com/p/why-are -our-fourth-graders-on-pornhub/.

38. Hogben, "I Had a Helicopter Mom."

39. Laura McKowen (@laura_mckowen), "If you think having uncomfortable conversations is hard," Instagram, January 23, 2025, https://www.instagram.com/p/DFLHqIvTBo9/. Emphasis original.

Chapter 6: Habit 5: Diligently Prevent Harm

1. L. David Perry, "The Impact of Pornography on Children," American College of Pediatricians, August 2024, https://acpeds.org/the-impact -of-pornography-on-children/.

2. Protect Young Eyes (@protectyoungeyes), "Great Questions from PYE Parents," Instagram, August 27, 2024, https://www.instagram.com/p /C_LjXb4Rqd7/.

3. "Talk, Trust, and Trade-Offs: How and Why Teens Use AI Companions," Common Sense, July 16, 2025, https://www .commonsensemedia.org/research/talk-trust-and-trade-offs-how-and -why-teens-use-ai-companions/.

4. "What Are AI Agents?," IBM, accessed December 5, 2025, https://www
.ibm.com/think/topics/ai-agents/.

5. "AI Companions Are Powerful. Here's Your Complete Guide," Protect
Young Eyes, August 13, 2025, https://www.protectyoungeyes.com/blog
-articles/complete-guide-to-ai-companions/.

6. **Trigger warning—sexual content:** "Create Your Own AI Girlfriend,"
Fantasy GF, accessed December 5, 2025, https://fantasygf.com/create
-ai-girl/.

7. "The Complete Guide to Deepfakes and AI for Caregivers," Protect
Young Eyes, January 8, 2024, https://www.protectyoungeyes.com/blog
-articles/ultimate-guide-to-ai-and-deepfakes-for-caregivers/.

8. "The Complete Guide to Deepfakes."

9. Rob Kuznia, Allison Gordon, and Ed Lavandera, "'You're Not Rushing.
You're Just Ready': Parents Say ChatGPT Encouraged Son to Kill
Himself," CNN, November 20, 2025, https://www.cnn.com/2025/11/06
/us/openai-chatgpt-suicide-lawsuit-invs-vis/.

10. Alyssa Goldberg, "Her 14-Year-Old Was Seduced by a Character.AI Bot.
She Says It Cost Him His Life," *USA Today*, October 20, 2025, https://
www.usatoday.com/story/life/health-wellness/2025/10/20/character
-ai-chatbot-relationships-teenagers/86745562007/.

11. Nitasha Tiku and Kevin Schaul, "74 Suicide Warnings and 243
Mentions of Hanging: What ChatGPT Said to a Suicidal Teen,"
Washington Post, December 27, 2025, https://www.washingtonpost
.com/technology/2025/12/27/chatgpt-suicide-openai-raine/.

12. Olivia Young, "Colorado Family Sues AI Chatbot Company After
Daughter's Suicide: 'My Child Should Be Here,'" CBS News, October 2,
2025, https://www.cbsnews.com/colorado/news/lawsuit-characterai
-chatbot-colorado-suicide/.

13. Anna Betts, "ChatGPT Accused of Acting as 'Suicide Coach' in Series
of US Lawsuits," *The Guardian*, November 7, 2025, https://www
.theguardian.com/technology/2025/nov/07/chatgpt-lawsuit-suicide
-coach/.

14. Michael B. Robb and Supreet Mann, *Talk, Trust, and Trade-Offs: How
and Why Teens Use AI Companions* (Common Sense Media, 2025), 2,

https://www.commonsensemedia.org/sites/default/files/research
/report/talk-trust-and-trade-offs_2025_web.pdf.

15. Protect Young Eyes (@protectyoungeyes), "AI chatbots, like ChatGPT,
are dangerous," Instagram, December 13, 2025, https://www
.instagram.com/reel/DSNSoTmjSee/.

16. R. J. Cross and Rory Erlich, "Alilo's 'Smart AI Bunny' Will Discuss
Inappropriate Topics," PIRG, December 2025, https://pirg.org/edfund
/wp-content/uploads/2025/12/PIRG-addendum-Alilo-Smart-AI
-Bunny-findings.pdf.

17. Cindy Tran, "Parents of the Year! Couple Whose Three Kids Refused
to Go on Their 'Boring' Road Trip Leave Thousands in Stitches After
Taking the MODEM with Them Instead," *Daily Mail*, January 13, 2020,
https://www.dailymail.co.uk/femail/article-7880465/Parents-Cassie
-Chris-three-kids-refused-road-trip-MODEM-instead.html/.

18. Protect Young Eyes (@protectyoungeyes), "We talk about routers a lot
at Protect Young Eyes," Instagram, February 21, 2024, https://www
.instagram.com/reel/C3oe5QMtj0x/=.

19. "The Ultimate Guide to Understanding Routers," Protect Young Eyes,
accessed December 5, 2025, https://www.protectyoungeyes.com
/devices/the-ultimate-guide-to-understanding-routers/.

20. Nick Lawler, "Piper Sandler Completes 50th Semi-Annual Teen
Survey," Piper Sandler, October 9, 2025, https://www.pipersandler.com
/news/piper-sandler-completes-50th-semi-annual-teen-survey/.

21. "The Complete Guide to Apple iPhone and iPad Set-Up and Parental
Controls," Protect Young Eyes, accessed December 5, 2025, https://
www.protectyoungeyes.com/devices/apple-ios-iphone-ipad-parental
-controls/.

22. "12 Ingenious iOS Screen Time Hacks (and How to Beat Them!),"
Protect Young Eyes, October 20, 2024, https://www.protectyoungeyes
.com/blog-articles/12-ingenious-screen-time-hacks-how-to-beat
-them/.

23. Mike Peterson, "Your iPhone Is 120 Million Times+ More Powerful
Than the Computer That Sent Men to the Moon," iDrop News, July 18,
2019, https://www.idropnews.com/news/your-iphone-is-120-million

-times-more-powerful-than-the-computer-that-sent-men-to-the
-moon/112146/.

24. "3 Reasons to Turn Off (Disable) the App Store," Protect Young Eyes,
January 16, 2023, https://www.protectyoungeyes.com/blog-articles/3
-reasons-turn-off-disable-app-store/.

25. "AI Companions Are Powerful. Here's Your Complete Guide," Protect
Young Eyes, August 13, 2025, https://www.protectyoungeyes.com/blog
-articles/complete-guide-to-ai-companions/.

26. Andrea Blanco, "Teen Boys at New Jersey School Accused of Creating
AI Deepfake Nudes of Female Classmates," *The Independent*,
November 2, 2023, https://www.independent.co.uk/news/deepfake
-nude-westfield-high-school-nj-b2440793.html/.

27. Heather Chen and Kathleen Magramo, "Finance Worker Pays Out $25
Million After Video Call with Deepfake 'Chief Financial Officer,'" CNN,
February 4, 2024, https://www.cnn.com/2024/02/04/asia/deepfake-cfo
-scam-hong-kong-intl-hnk/.

28. Blanco, "Teen Boys at New Jersey School Accused."

29. Kalie Walker, "AI 'Deepfakes': A Disturbing Trend in School
Cyberbullying," NEA Today, April 10, 2025, https://www.nea.org
/nea-today/all-news-articles/ai-deepfakes-disturbing-trend-school
-cyberbullying/.

30. "5 Most Dangerous Places for Kids to Be Online," Protect Young Eyes,
August 7, 2023, https://www.protectyoungeyes.com/blog-articles/5
-most-dangerous-places-for-kids-to-be-online/.

31. Emma Henderson Vaughan, "NCMEC Releases New Data: 2024 in
Numbers," National Center for Missing & Exploited Children, May 8,
2025, https://www.missingkids.org/blog/2025/ncmec-releases-new
-data-2024-in-numbers/.

32. Katie McQue, "BM Boys: The Nigerian Sextortion Network Hiding
in Plain Sight on TikTok," *The Guardian*, May 11, 2025, https://www
.theguardian.com/us-news/2025/may/11/sextortion-nigeria-bm-boys
-tiktok/.

33. Alana Ray and Nicola Henry, "Sextortion: A Scoping Review," *Trauma,
Violence, & Abuse* 26, no. 1 (2025): 138–55, https://pubmed.ncbi.nlm
.nih.gov/39323232/.

34. See https://takeitdown.ncmec.org/ for more information on this tool.

35. Shannon Bond, "Instagram Unveils New Teen Safety Tools Ahead of Senate Hearing," NPR, December 7, 2021, https://www.npr.org/2021/12/07/1061808098/instagram-teens-safety-tools/.

36. Charlotte Alter, "Instagram Promised to Become Safer for Teens. Researchers Say It's Not Working," *Time*, October 9, 2025, https://time.com/7324544/instagram-teen-accounts-flawed/.

37. Mark Sellman, "Four-Year-Olds 'Exploited' by Tech Giants' App Store Age Ratings," *The Times*, June 30, 2025, https://www.thetimes.com/uk/technology-uk/article/four-year-olds-exploited-by-tech-giants-app-store-age-ratings-6txf0z0zr/.

38. Sezlou, "Inappropriate Ads in Kids Games," Apple Support Community, August 7, 2019, https://discussions.apple.com/thread/250539858?sortBy=rank.

39. "Teen Spends $20,000 of Mother's Money on Twitch and Fortnite," 7News, July 22, 2020, https://7news.com.au/technology/teen-spends-20000-of-mothers-money-on-twitch-and-fortnite-c-1183967/.

40. Carpluvbirds, "How to Avoid Inappropriate Ads in Kids Games on iPhone?," Apple Community, February 15, 2025, https://discussions.apple.com/thread/255972997.

Chapter 7: Building a Tech-Ready World

1. "Fall 2025 Piper Sandler Teen Survey," Piper Sandler, accessed December 5, 2025, https://www.pipersandler.com/teens/.

2. Christopher (Chris) McKenna, testimony in "Protecting Innocence in a Digital World," Senate Committee on the Judiciary, July 9, 2019, https://www.judiciary.senate.gov/imo/media/doc/McKenna%20Testimony.pdf.

3. "Attractive Nuisance Doctrine," Cornell Law School Legal Information Institute, accessed December 5, 2025, https://www.law.cornell.edu/wex/attractive_nuisance_doctrine/.

4. "S.B. 142 App Store Accountability Act," Utah State Legislature, March 26, 2025, https://le.utah.gov/~2025/bills/static/SB0142.html/.

5. "H.B. No. 1181," Texas Legislature Online, September 1, 2023, https://capitol.texas.gov/tlodocs/88R/billtext/html/HB01181H.htm.

6. "Kids Online Safety Act," Common Sense, accessed December 5, 2025, https://www.commonsensemedia.org/sites/default/files/featured-content/files/kosa-one-pager.pdf.

7. "California Age-Appropriate Design Code Act," Common Sense, accessed December 5, 2025, https://www.commonsensemedia.org/sites/default/files/featured-content/files/ca-design-code-one-pager-2023-1.pdf.

8. "Hawley Bill to Protect Children from AI Chatbots Gains New Cosponsors," Josh Hawley, U.S. Senator for Missouri, December 10, 2025, https://www.hawley.senate.gov/hawley-bill-to-protect-children-from-ai-chatbots-gains-new-cosponsors/.

9. "State Policies," The Anxious Generation, accessed December 5, 2025, https://www.anxiousgeneration.com/policy-state-map/.

10. "Phone-Free and Low-Tech Schools," Protect Young Eyes, accessed December 5, 2025, https://www.protectyoungeyes.com/phone-free-low-tech-schools/.

11. Protect Young Eyes (@protectyoungeyes), "I'm a High Schooler. AI Is Demolishing My Education," Instagram, September 8, 2025, https://www.instagram.com/p/DOXMbLtDIBs/.

12. Jon Haidt, "The Teen Mental Illness Epidemic Began Around 2012," After Babel, February 8, 2023, https://www.afterbabel.com/p/the-teen-mental-illness-epidemic/.

13. Ana J. Bridges, Robert Wosnitzer, Erica Scharrer, Chyng Sun, and Rachael Liberman, "Aggression and Sexual Behavior in Best-Selling Pornography Videos: A Content Analysis Update," *Violence Against Women* 16, no. 10 (2010): 1065–85, https://pubmed.ncbi.nlm.nih.gov/20980228/.

14. Chris McKenna, "It's difficult to surprise me," LinkedIn, December 2024, https://www.linkedin.com/posts/chris-mckenna-75962211_delayistheway-onepreciouschildhood-activity-7266812536681828352-1gfU/.

15. Jonathan Haidt, *The Anxious Generation: How the Great Rewiring of Childhood Is Causing an Epidemic of Mental Illness* (Penguin, 2024), 211.

16. Julie Hook, "Brainrot: What Happens When an Ancient Brain Meets a Modern World," Medium, December 12, 2025, https://medium.com/@

jnhook/brainrot-what-happens-when-an-ancient-brain-meets-a
-modern-world-50dd281eec03/.

17. "Aligned Organizations," The Anxious Generation, accessed December 5, 2025, https://www.anxiousgeneration.com/aligned-orgs/.

18. See https://www.smartphonefreechildhood.org/ for a great example of how parents are coming together to protect their kids' childhood.

19. "Phone-Free and Low-Tech Schools," Protect Young Eyes, accessed December 5, 2025, https://www.protectyoungeyes.com/phone-free-low-tech-schools/.

20. Chris McKenna, "My School Board Script About Phones, Chromebooks, and AI," Almost Always Analog, August 5, 2025, https://chriswmckenna.substack.com/p/my-school-board-script-about-phones/.

21. "Aligned Organizations."

Appendix 1: How to Talk About Porn with Your Kid

1. "What's the Average Age of a Child's First Exposure to Porn?," Fight the New Drug, accessed December 5, 2025, https://fightthenewdrug.org/real-average-age-of-first-exposure/.

2. Linda Jeffries, "My 13-Year-Old Son Struggles with Pornography. What Should I Do?," Eternal Perspective Ministries, July 20, 2011, https://www.epm.org/resources/2011/Jul/20/my-13-year-old-son-struggles-pornography-what-shou/.

Appendix 2: Is It Too Late to Delay? What If My Kids Already Have Tech?

1. Abby Alger, "You Gave Your Kid Social Media and Regret It. Now What?," *Gabb Now* (blog), March 26, 2025, https://gabb.com/blog/how-to-undo-social-media/.

2. "Permanently Delete or Deactivate Your Instagram Account," Instagram Help Center, accessed December 5, 2025, https://help.instagram.com/370452623149242/.

3. "How Do I Deactivate or Delete My Snapchat Account?," Snapchat, accessed December 5, 2025, https://help.snapchat.com/hc/en-us/articles/7012328360596-How-do-I-deactivate-or-delete-my-Snapchat-account/.

4. "How to Deactivate Your Account," X Help Center, accessed December 5, 2025, https://help.x.com/en/managing-your-account/how-to-deactivate-x-account/.

5. "Delete Your Account," TikTok, accessed December 5, 2025, https://support.tiktok.com/en/account-and-privacy/deleting-an-account/deleting-an-account/.

6. "Permanently Delete Your Facebook Account," Facebook Help Center, accessed December 5, 2025, https://www.facebook.com/help/224562897555674/.

7. "The Protect Young Eyes Community," Protect Young Eyes, accessed January 7, 2026, https://www.protectyoungeyes.com/the-table/.

Appendix 3: Recommended Tech Resources

1. "Protect Young Eyes Recommends the Bark Phone," Bark, accessed December 5, 2025, https://www.bark.us/learn/bark-phone-pye/.

2. "YouTube Kids," Protect Young Eyes, accessed December 5, 2025, https://www.protectyoungeyes.com/apps/youtube-kids-parental-controls/.

3. "Teens and Pornography," Common Sense, 2022, https://www.commonsensemedia.org/sites/default/files/research/report/2022-teens-and-pornography-final-web.pdf.

4. "6 Tech Questions to Ask Principals," Protect Young Eyes, August 12, 2025, https://www.protectyoungeyes.com/blog-articles/6-tech-questions-to-ask-every-school-principal/.

5. Tristan Harris, "Why AI Is Our Ultimate Test and Greatest Invitation," posted May 1, 2025 by TED, YouTube, 15 min., 15 sec., https://www.youtube.com/watch?v=6kPHnl-RsVI/.

About the Author

Chris McKenna is a national leader in digital wellness and child online safety. As founder and CEO of Protect Young Eyes (PYE), he equips families, schools, and organizations to create safer digital spaces. He also serves as president of The Better Tech Project, a non-profit dedicated to helping students thrive in a digital world.

Chris's 2019 US Senate testimony sparked sustained conversations around child-protection legislation and responsible technology design. At the 2024 and 2025 World Economic Forum he facilitated discussions about the global phone-free movement in schools, strategies for protecting kids at home, and policies that hold technology companies accountable. His advocacy earned PYE the Dignity Defense Alert Award from the National Center on Sexual Exploitation and the Child Safety Award from the PHASE Alliance.

Alongside his team, Chris travels globally to deliver digital-safety education and consult with schools and church communities. He is featured in the documentary *Childhood 2.0*, viewed by millions worldwide.

Chris, Andrea, their kids, and their dogs have always lived in Michigan. Connect with Chris at https://www.protectyoungeyes.com.